Crossing Your River

Strategies to Achieve Your DREAM

Joshua Marshman

Contents

Introduction, Crossing the River

Dream It, Achieve It

The DREAM Method for Creating Predictable Success

Book Overview

"Crossing Your River" is an easy-to-understand compilation of proven strategies to help you achieve your dreams which are waiting for you just on the other side of the river. These proven systems have helped individuals trying to get to the next level or looking to escape from a funk as well as provided a comprehensive guide for small business owners who want to master the art of goal setting and strategies to grow their business.

This book introduces the DREAM Method, a step-by-step approach to maximizing productivity and getting the results you have always dreamed of.

D – Define Your Goals

R – Remove Your Obstacles

E – Enhance Your Strategies

A – Automate Your Systems

M – Multiply Your Growth

Define Your Goals

In this book, you will learn the importance of goal setting and how to set SMART goals that are specific, measurable, attainable, relevant, and time-bound. You will discover how the power of visualization can help you visualize your goals and create an action plan to turn your dreams into reality. *These goals are represented by the other side of the river.*

Remove Your Obstacles

The book also focuses on removing obstacles that may hinder your progress, such as limiting beliefs, procrastination, and stress. *These obstacles can be represented by fallen debris or dangerous rapids* that you can't cross until you remove them or navigate around them. You will learn strategies to overcome these challenges and build a supportive network that will help you bridge the gap to staying motivated and focused.

Enhance Your Strategies

Additionally, the book provides strategies to enhance your planning, decision-making, communication, and problem-solving skills to ensure success in your business endeavors. *These supportive networks and strategies are the stepping stones that add up to create a pathway for you to get across.* Once you've proven that it's possible to get across the river on your stepping stones, then you can begin to solidify the pathway into a bridge.

Automate Your Systems

This optimized bridge becomes the system you use to predictably access your goal when you want to. "Crossing Your River" emphasizes the importance of automating your systems to streamline business processes and increase efficiency. You will learn how to implement technology and software solutions, outsource tasks, and create efficient workflows. The book also delves into strategies for multiplying your growth, expanding your customer base, scaling your operations, and diversifying your product or service offerings.

Multiply Your Growth

Lastly, once you have proven to yourself that you can cross the river once by building a predictable bridge you can multiply the growth along your journey. This book provides insights into creating worry-free wealth through financial planning, budgeting, investing, and wealth management. You will learn how to build multiple streams of income, protect your assets, and manage risks effectively. The book concludes with guidance on reviewing your progress, maintaining motivation, taking action, and inspiring others to achieve their dreams.

"Crossing Your River" is a must-read for individuals and small business owners who are ready to take their journey to new heights. It aims to create a system for overcoming obstacles and accomplishing goals that you can go back to time and time again to turn your dreams into reality.

About the Author

For those of you who don't know me, my name is
Joshua Marshman. For those of you who do know me,
my name is still Joshua Marshman.

Joshua Marshman is an executive business coach, certified Agile
Leader, loving husband & father of 3 wonderful kids, with a passion
for helping people face their challenges and reach their goals.

After graduating from the University of Colorado with a degree
in Aerospace Engineering and a specialty in systems management,
Joshua spent 8 years leading mission trips as a youth pastor all over the
world. Many of these trips were centered on empowering individuals
to develop leadership skills that they could take back to their communities. He strives to equip others with how to use their resources
more effectively. His desire to encourage people toward greatness and
help them reach their goals has been an integral part of his personal
and professional life. He has taken his decades of leadership experience
to develop this concise DREAM method and help people everywhere
cross their rivers.

In every workplace he has been a part of, he has created a rich culture of acceptance and empowerment, listening to the circumstances

and dreams of people and developing efficient strategies to help them meet their fullest potential. With his clients he works to cultivate a longterm relationship focused on their long-term interests.

Joshua is an avid hiker, climber and skier. He's no stranger to facing rivers and mountains that at first seem too hard to cross. He has summited many of the tallest peaks in the Rocky Mountains, travelled in over 30+ countries, and even cycled over 4000 miles across China filming a documentary called "Overcoming Mountains". Through all of these adventures, he has learned how powerful the right tools, guidance (or leadership), motivation, and belief in yourself can be to succeed in reaching the unthinkable.

1 Introduction to Goal Mastery

1.1 Understanding the Importance of Goal Setting

Setting goals is a fundamental aspect of achieving success in any endeavor, and it is especially crucial for individuals and small business owners. Without clear goals, it becomes challenging to stay focused, and motivated, and make progress toward your desired outcomes. In this section, we will explore the importance of goal setting and how it can significantly impact the success of your small business.

1.1.1 Defining Goals

Before delving into the significance of goal setting, it is essential to understand what goals are. Goals are the specific objectives or targets that you aim to achieve within a defined timeframe. They provide direction, purpose, and a roadmap for your business. By setting clear and measurable goals, you can effectively track your progress and make necessary adjustments along the way.

1.1.2 Clarity and Focus

One of the primary benefits of goal setting is that it brings clarity and focus to your business. When you have a clear vision of what you want to achieve, it becomes easier to prioritize tasks, make decisions, and allocate resources effectively. Goals act as a guiding light, helping you stay on track and avoid getting sidetracked by distractions or irrelevant activities.

1.1.3 Motivation and Commitment

Setting goals provides you with a sense of purpose and motivation. When you have a clear target in mind, you are more likely to be driven to take action and work toward its attainment. Goals create a sense of urgency and commitment, pushing you to go the extra mile and overcome obstacles that may come your way. They serve as a constant reminder of why you started your business and what you aspire to achieve.

1.1.4 Measuring Progress

Goal setting allows you to measure your progress and evaluate your performance. By setting specific and measurable goals, you can track your achievements and identify areas where you may need to improve. Regularly monitoring your progress helps you stay accountable and make necessary adjustments to your strategies or actions. It also provides a sense of accomplishment as you reach milestones and move closer to your ultimate objectives.

1.1.5 Setting Realistic Expectations

When setting goals, it is crucial to strike a balance between ambition and realism. While it is essential to aim high and challenge yourself, setting unrealistic goals can lead to frustration and demotivation. By setting realistic and achievable goals, you set yourself up for success and maintain a positive mindset throughout your journey. Realistic goals also help you manage your resources effectively and avoid burnout.

1.1.6 Enhancing Decision-Making

Goal setting plays a vital role in enhancing your decision-making process. When faced with various options or opportunities, having clear goals allows you to evaluate them based on their alignment with your objectives. Goals act as a filter, helping you make informed decisions that are in line with your long-term vision. This focus on goal alignment ensures that your actions contribute to the overall success of your business.

1.1.7 Building Confidence and Resilience

As a small business owner, you will inevitably face challenges and setbacks along the way. However, having well-defined goals can help you build confidence and resilience in the face of adversity. When you encounter obstacles, your goals serve as a reminder of your capabilities and the progress you have already made. They provide the motivation to persevere and find alternative solutions to overcome challenges.

1.1.8 Alignment and Collaboration

Goal setting is not limited to individual efforts; it also plays a crucial role in aligning and collaborating with your team. When everyone in your organization is aware of the goals and understands their role in achieving them, it fosters a sense of unity and shared purpose. Clear goals provide a common language and direction, enabling effective communication, collaboration, and synergy among team members.

1.1.9 Continuous Improvement

Setting goals is not a one-time activity; it is an ongoing process of continuous improvement. As you achieve your goals, you can set new ones that push you further and help you grow your business. By regularly reviewing and updating your goals, you ensure that your business stays relevant, adaptable, and responsive to changing market conditions. Goal setting encourages innovation and keeps you ahead of the competition.

1.1.10 Conclusion

In conclusion, goal setting is a critical component of small business success. It provides clarity, focus, motivation, and a roadmap for achieving your desired outcomes. By setting clear and measurable goals, you can measure your progress, make informed decisions, build confidence, and foster collaboration within your team. Goal setting is an ongoing process that promotes continuous improvement and ensures the long-term success of your small business. In the next section, we will explore the power of visualization and how it can enhance your goal-setting journey.

1.2 The Power of Visualization

Visualization is a powerful tool that can help small business owners achieve their goals and dreams. It involves creating vivid mental images of what you want to achieve and experiencing the emotions associated with that success. By visualizing your goals, you can tap into the power of your subconscious mind and align your thoughts, beliefs, and actions with your desired outcomes.

1.2.1 The Science Behind Visualization

The concept of visualization is not just a new age or mystical practice; it is backed by scientific research. Studies have shown that when we visualize an action or outcome, our brain activates the same neural pathways as when we actually perform that action. This means that by vividly imagining yourself achieving your goals, you are training your brain to believe that it is possible and increasing your chances of success.

Visualization also helps to activate the reticular activating system (RAS) in our brain. The RAS acts as a filter, allowing us to focus on the information that is most relevant to us. When we visualize our goals, we are programming our RAS to pay attention to opportunities and resources that can help us achieve those goals. This heightened awareness allows us to spot opportunities that we may have otherwise missed.

1.2.2 The Benefits of Visualization

1. Clarifies Your Goals: Visualization helps you gain clarity about what you truly want to achieve. By creating a clear mental image of your goals, you can define them more precisely and understand the steps needed to accomplish them.

2. Boosts Motivation: When you visualize yourself achieving your goals, you tap into the emotions associated with that success. This emotional connection fuels your motivation and determination to take action and overcome obstacles.

3. Increases Confidence: Visualization helps build confidence by allowing you to see yourself as a successful business owner. By repeatedly visualizing your success, you reinforce positive beliefs about your abilities and increase your self-confidence.

4. Enhances Focus and Concentration: When you visualize your goals, you train your mind to focus on what is important. This increased focus and concentration enable you to prioritize tasks and make better decisions that align with your goals.

5. Reduces Stress and Anxiety: Visualization can be a powerful stress management tool. By visualizing yourself successfully navigating challenges and achieving your goals, you can reduce stress and anxiety levels. This positive mindset helps you stay calm and focused, even in high-pressure situations.

6. Improves Performance: Athletes have long used visualization techniques to improve their performance. By visualizing yourself successfully completing tasks and achieving your

goals, you can enhance your skills and increase your chances of success.

1.2.3 How to Practice Visualization

1. **Create a Quiet Space**: Find a quiet and comfortable space where you can relax and focus without distractions. This could be a quiet room in your home or a peaceful outdoor setting.

2. **Set Clear Goals**: Before you begin visualizing, clearly define your goals. Be specific about what you want to achieve and the timeline for accomplishing it.

3. **Use All Your Senses**: Engage all your senses when visualizing your goals. Imagine how it feels, looks, sounds, smells, and even tastes to achieve your desired outcomes. The more vivid and detailed your visualization, the more powerful it becomes.

4. **Visualize Step-by-Step**: Break down your goals into smaller, manageable steps, and visualize yourself successfully completing each step. This will help you build momentum and confidence as you progress toward your ultimate goal.

5. **Practice Regularly**: Make visualization a daily practice. Set aside dedicated time each day to visualize your goals and immerse yourself in the emotions associated with your success. The more you practice, the more effective your visualization becomes.

6. **Combine Visualization with Action**: Visualization alone is not enough; it must be accompanied by action. Use your visualization as a guide to take inspired action toward your goals. Take consistent steps toward your vision, and you will see your dreams turn into reality.

1.2.4 Real-Life Examples of Visualization in Action

Many successful entrepreneurs and business leaders attribute their achievements to the power of visualization. Here are a few examples:

1. Oprah Winfrey: Oprah Winfrey, one of the most influential media moguls, has spoken about how she used visualization to manifest her success. She visualized herself hosting her own talk show and becoming a household name long before it happened.

2. Richard Branson: The founder of Virgin Group, Richard Branson, is known for his visualization techniques. He visualized himself as a successful entrepreneur and used that vision to guide his actions and decisions.

3. Jim Carrey: Before becoming a famous actor, Jim Carrey wrote himself a check for $10 million for "acting services rendered" and dated it for Thanksgiving 1995. He carried that check in his wallet and visualized himself receiving that amount. In 1994, he landed a role in the movie "Dumb and Dumber" and earned exactly $10 million.

These examples demonstrate the power of visualization in achieving extraordinary success. By harnessing the power of your mind and visualizing your goals, you can create a roadmap for success and turn your dreams into reality.

Visualization is a valuable tool that can help small business owners overcome obstacles, stay focused, and achieve their goals. By incorporating visualization into your goal mastery journey, you can unlock your full potential and create the business and life you have always dreamed of.

1.3 Setting SMART Goals

Setting goals is an essential step in achieving success, both personally and professionally. As a small business owner, it is crucial to have a clear vision of what you want to accomplish and a roadmap to guide you along the way. One effective approach to goal setting is using the SMART goals framework. SMART stands for Specific, Measurable, Achievable, Relevant, and Time-bound. In this section, we will explore how to set SMART goals and why they are important for small business success.

1.3.1 Specific

When setting goals, it is important to be specific about what you want to achieve. Vague or general goals can be difficult to measure and track progress. By clearly defining your objectives, you can focus your efforts and increase your chances of success. For example, instead of setting a goal to "increase sales," a specific goal would be to "increase sales by 20% in the next quarter."

1.3.2 Measurable

Measuring progress is essential to stay on track and evaluate the effectiveness of your efforts. By setting measurable goals, you can quantify your progress and determine whether you are moving in the right direction. Measurable goals are often expressed in terms of numbers, percentages, or other quantifiable metrics. For instance, a measurable goal could be to "acquire 100 new customers within the next six months."

1.3.3 Achievable

While it is important to set ambitious goals, they should also be realistic and attainable. Setting goals that are too far out of reach can lead to frustration and demotivation. Consider your available resources, skills, and capabilities when setting goals. It is better to set smaller, achievable goals that can be built upon over time. For example, if you are a small business owner just starting out, setting a goal to "generate $1 million in revenue within the first year" may not be realistic. Instead, a more achievable goal could be to "generate $100,000 in revenue within the first year."

1.3.4 Relevant

Relevance is an important aspect of goal setting. Your goals should align with your overall vision and mission as a small business owner. They should be relevant to your industry, market, and target audience. Setting goals that are not relevant to your business can lead to wasted time and resources. Ensure that your goals contribute to the growth and success of your business. For example, if your business is in the technology sector, setting a goal to "attend a marketing conference" may not be as relevant as setting a goal to "launch a new digital marketing campaign."

1.3.5 Time-bound

Setting a deadline for your goals is crucial to create a sense of urgency and accountability. Without a timeframe, goals can easily be pushed aside or forgotten. By setting specific timeframes, you can prioritize your tasks and allocate resources accordingly. Time-bound goals help you stay focused and motivated. For example, instead of setting a goal to "improve customer service," a time-bound goal would be to "reduce customer response time to within 24 hours by the end of the month."

Why SMART Goals are Important for Small Business Success

Setting SMART goals is essential for small business success for several reasons. Firstly, SMART goals provide clarity and direction. By clearly defining your objectives, you can align your actions and decisions with your desired outcomes. This clarity helps you stay focused and avoid distractions.

Secondly, SMART goals enable you to measure progress and track your achievements. By setting specific and measurable goals, you can monitor your progress and make adjustments as needed. This allows you to stay on track and make informed decisions based on real-time data.

Thirdly, SMART goals promote accountability and motivation. When you set time-bound goals, you create a sense of urgency and commitment. This accountability drives you to take action and stay motivated, even when faced with challenges or setbacks.

Lastly, SMART goals help you prioritize your efforts and allocate resources effectively. By setting achievable and relevant goals, you can identify the most important tasks and allocate your time, energy, and resources accordingly. This ensures that you are working on the tasks that will have the greatest impact on your business.

In conclusion, setting SMART goals is a powerful tool for small business owners to maximize their productivity and achieve the results they have dreamed of. By following the SMART framework and setting specific, measurable, achievable, relevant, and time-bound goals, you can create a roadmap for success and stay on track toward your desired outcomes. Remember, goal mastery is not just about setting goals but also about taking consistent action and adapting your strategies along the way.

1.4 Creating an Action Plan

Once you have set your goals using the SMART framework, it is essential to create an action plan to guide you toward achieving them. An action plan is a roadmap that outlines the specific steps you need to take to reach your goals. It helps you stay organized, focused, and motivated throughout your journey.

1.4.1 Breaking Down Your Goals

To create an effective action plan, start by breaking down your goals into smaller, manageable tasks. This process allows you to see the bigger picture while also identifying the specific actions required to achieve each goal. By breaking down your goals, you can tackle them one step at a time, making them less overwhelming and more attainable.

Begin by listing all the tasks that need to be completed to achieve each goal. Be as specific as possible and include any deadlines or milestones that need to be met. For example, if your goal is to increase your customer base by 20% within six months, your tasks may include conducting market research, developing a marketing strategy, implementing targeted advertising campaigns, and tracking customer acquisition metrics.

1.4.2 Prioritizing Your Tasks

Once you have identified all the tasks necessary to achieve your goals, it is crucial to prioritize them. Not all tasks are created equal, and some may have a more significant impact on your overall success than others. Prioritizing your tasks ensures that you focus your time and energy on the most critical activities that will drive you closer to your goals.

Consider the urgency and importance of each task when prioritizing. Urgent tasks are those that require immediate attention, while important tasks contribute directly to the achievement of your goals. Use a prioritization matrix or a simple numbering system to rank your tasks based on their urgency and importance. This will help you allocate your resources effectively and ensure that you are working on the most critical tasks first.

1.4.3 Setting Deadlines

Setting deadlines for each task is essential to keep yourself accountable and maintain momentum toward your goals. Without deadlines, tasks can easily be pushed aside or delayed, resulting in a lack of progress. By assigning specific deadlines to each task, you create a sense of urgency and ensure that you stay on track.

When setting deadlines, be realistic and consider the time and resources required to complete each task. Avoid setting overly ambitious deadlines that may lead to burnout or compromise the quality of your work. Break down larger tasks into smaller subtasks and assign deadlines accordingly. This will help you manage your time effectively and prevent overwhelm.

1.4.4 Allocating Resources

As you create your action plan, consider the resources you will need to accomplish each task. Resources can include time, money, equipment, and personnel. Assess what resources are available to you and determine if any additional resources need to be acquired or allocated.

Allocate your resources strategically, ensuring that they are aligned with the priority of each task. If a task requires a significant investment of time or money, make sure you have the necessary resources available before starting. If you need assistance or expertise, consider outsourcing or delegating certain tasks to free up your time and focus on activities that require your unique skills and knowledge.

1.4.5 Tracking Progress

To stay motivated and ensure that you are making progress toward your goals, it is crucial to track your progress regularly. Set up a system to monitor and measure the completion of each task and the overall progress toward your goals. This can be as simple as using a spreadsheet or task management software to track completed tasks, deadlines, and milestones.

Regularly review your action plan and update it as needed. As you make progress, you may encounter new opportunities or challenges that require adjustments to your plan. By regularly reviewing and updating your action plan, you can adapt to changing circumstances and stay on course toward achieving your goals.

1.4.6 Celebrating Milestones

As you complete tasks and reach milestones along your journey, take the time to celebrate your achievements. Celebrating milestones not only boosts morale but also reinforces your commitment to your goals. It provides a sense of accomplishment and motivates you to continue working toward your larger objectives.

Celebrate milestones in a way that is meaningful to you. It could be as simple as treating yourself to a small reward or sharing your achievements with your support network. Recognize the progress you have made and acknowledge the effort and dedication you have put into reaching each milestone. Celebrating milestones creates positive momentum and fuels your motivation to keep pushing forward.

In conclusion, creating an action plan is a crucial step in goal mastery for small business owners. By breaking down your goals, prioritizing tasks, setting deadlines, allocating resources, tracking progress, and celebrating milestones, you can maximize your productivity and increase your chances of achieving the results you have dreamed of. Remember, an action plan is not set in stone and can be adjusted as needed. Stay flexible, stay focused, and keep taking action toward your goals.

Chapter Two

2 Defining Your Goals

Sometimes the best way to know where you want to
be is to acknowledge where you don't want to stay.

2.1 Identifying Your Passions and Values

In order to set meaningful and fulfilling goals for your small business, it is essential to first identify your passions and values. Your passions are the things that ignite your enthusiasm and bring you joy, while your values are the principles and beliefs that guide your actions and decisions. When you align your goals with your passions and values, you create a strong foundation for success and fulfillment.

Understanding Your Passions

Passions are the driving force behind your motivation and dedication. They are the activities or areas of interest that make you feel alive and energized. Identifying your passions is crucial because when you are passionate about something, you are more likely to put in the necessary effort and overcome obstacles to achieve your goals.

To identify your passions, take some time for self-reflection. Ask yourself the following questions:

1. What activities do I enjoy doing the most?

2. What topics or subjects do I find myself constantly reading or learning about?

3. What hobbies or interests do I pursue in my free time?

4. What tasks or projects do I lose track of time while working on?

5. What activities make me feel fulfilled and satisfied?

By answering these questions honestly, you can gain insight into the activities and areas of interest that bring you joy and fulfillment. These are the areas where your passions lie.

Clarifying Your Values

Values are the guiding principles that shape your behavior and decision-making. They are the beliefs and ideals that are most important to you. When your goals align with your values, you create a sense of purpose and meaning in your work.

To clarify your values, consider the following:

1. What principles do I hold dear in both my personal and professional life?

2. What qualities do I admire in others?

3. What do I want to be known for?

4. What are the non-negotiables in my life and business?

By answering these questions, you can identify the values that are most important to you. These values will serve as a compass, guiding your decisions and actions as you work toward your goals.

Aligning Passions and Values with Business Goals

Once you have identified your passions and values, it is important to align them with your business goals. This alignment ensures that your goals are not only financially rewarding but also personally fulfilling.

To align your passions and values with your business goals, follow these steps:

1. Review your passions and values: Take a look at the passions and values you have identified and remind yourself of why they are important to you.

2. Evaluate your current business goals: Assess your existing goals and determine if they align with your passions and values. If they do not, consider revising or redefining your goals to better align with what truly matters to you.

3. Set new goals if necessary: If your current goals do not align with your passions and values, set new goals that do. Consider how you can incorporate your passions and values into your business strategy.

4. Create an action plan: Once you have identified your pas-

sions, values, and aligned goals, create a detailed action plan to achieve them. Break down your goals into smaller, manageable tasks and set deadlines for each task.

5. Stay committed: Remember that aligning your passions and values with your business goals is an ongoing process. Stay committed to your goals and regularly reassess them to ensure they continue to align with what truly matters to you.

By identifying your passions and values and aligning them with your business goals, you create a strong foundation for success and fulfillment. When your work is driven by your passions and guided by your values, you are more likely to stay motivated, overcome obstacles, and achieve the results you have dreamed of.

2.2 Setting Long-Term and Short-Term Goals

Setting goals is an essential step in achieving success in any endeavor, especially in the world of small business. Without clear goals, it becomes challenging to stay focused, motivated, and make progress toward your desired outcomes. In this section, we will explore the importance of setting both long-term and short-term goals and how they work together to propel your business forward.

2.2.1 The Significance of Long-Term Goals

Long-term goals provide a vision for your business's future. They are the big picture objectives that you aspire to achieve over an extended period, typically spanning several years. These goals serve as a guiding light, giving you direction and purpose. When setting long-term goals, it is crucial to consider your passions, values, and the ultimate vision you have for your business.

Long-term goals help you:

1. **Provide Clarity**: By defining your long-term goals, you gain clarity about where you want your business to be in the future. This clarity allows you to make informed decisions and align your actions with your desired outcomes.

2. **Stay Focused**: Long-term goals act as a compass, keeping you focused on the bigger picture. They help you avoid getting caught up in day-to-day tasks and distractions that may hinder your progress.

3. **Motivate and Inspire**: Having ambitious long-term goals can be highly motivating and inspiring. They push you to step out of your comfort zone, take calculated risks, and strive for excellence.

4. **Measure Progress**: Long-term goals provide a benchmark against which you can measure your progress. They allow you to track your achievements and make adjustments if necessary.

When setting long-term goals, it is essential to make them specific, measurable, achievable, relevant, and time-bound (SMART). This ensures that your goals are realistic and actionable, increasing the likelihood of success.

2.2.2 The Power of Short-Term Goals

While long-term goals provide the overarching vision, short-term goals are the stepping stones that lead you toward your desired outcomes. Short-term goals are smaller, more manageable objectives that you can achieve within a shorter timeframe, typically ranging from a few weeks to a few months.

Short-term goals offer several benefits:

1. **Immediate Progress**: Short-term goals allow you to experience a sense of accomplishment and progress more frequently. Achieving these smaller milestones boosts your confidence and motivates you to keep moving forward.

2. **Flexibility and Adaptability**: Short-term goals provide the flexibility to adjust your strategies and tactics as needed. They allow you to respond to changes in the market, industry, or business environment more effectively.

3. **Focus and Prioritization**: Short-term goals help you break down your long-term goals into actionable steps. By focusing on one goal at a time, you can prioritize your efforts and allocate resources accordingly.

4. **Feedback and Learning**: Short-term goals provide opportunities for feedback and learning. As you work toward these goals, you gain insights into what works and what doesn't, allowing you to refine your strategies and improve your performance.

When setting short-term goals, it is crucial to align them with your long-term goals. Each short-term goal should contribute to the overall vision and bring you closer to achieving your long-term objectives.

Additionally, short-term goals should also be SMART, ensuring they are specific, measurable, achievable, relevant, and time-bound.

2.2.3 The Synergy between Long-Term and Short-Term Goals

Long-term and short-term goals are not mutually exclusive; they work together in harmony to drive your business toward success. Long-term goals provide the vision and direction, while short-term goals provide the actionable steps to reach that vision.

The synergy between long-term and short-term goals can be seen in the following ways:

1. **Alignment**: Short-term goals should align with your long-term goals. Each short-term goal should contribute to the overall vision and bring you closer to achieving your long-term objectives.

2. **Progression**: Short-term goals act as milestones on the path toward your long-term goals. As you achieve each short-term goal, you make progress toward your ultimate vision.

3. **Adaptability**: Short-term goals allow you to adapt and adjust your strategies as needed to stay on track toward your long-term goals. They provide the flexibility to respond to changes and challenges along the way.

4. **Motivation**: Short-term goals provide a sense of achievement and progress, keeping you motivated and inspired to continue working toward your long-term goals.

To maximize the effectiveness of your goal-setting process, it is essential to regularly review and reassess both your long-term and short-term goals. As your business evolves and circumstances change, you may need to make adjustments to ensure your goals remain relevant and achievable.

In conclusion, setting both long-term and short-term goals is crucial for small business success. Long-term goals provide the vision and direction, while short-term goals offer the actionable steps to reach that vision. By aligning and integrating these goals, you can stay focused, motivated, and make consistent progress toward your desired outcomes.

2.3 Prioritizing Your Goals

Once you have identified your passions and values and set both long-term and short-term goals, the next step in the goal mastery process is to prioritize your goals. Prioritization is crucial because it allows you to focus your time, energy, and resources on the goals that are most important to you and your small business.

2.3.1 Assessing Importance and Urgency

To effectively prioritize your goals, it is essential to assess their importance and urgency. Importance refers to the significance and impact a goal has on your business and personal life, while urgency relates to the time sensitivity and deadlines associated with each goal.

Start by evaluating the importance of each goal. Consider how achieving a particular goal aligns with your overall vision and mission for your small business. Ask yourself questions such as:

- How will achieving this goal contribute to the growth and

success of my business?

- Does this goal align with my core values and long-term aspirations?

- Will accomplishing this goal have a positive impact on my customers, employees, or stakeholders?

Once you have assessed the importance of each goal, it's time to evaluate their urgency. Determine the deadlines or timeframes associated with each goal and consider any external factors that may influence their urgency. Ask yourself:

- Is there a specific deadline or timeframe for achieving this goal?

- Are there any external factors, such as market trends or industry changes, that make this goal time-sensitive?

- Will delaying the pursuit of this goal have negative consequences for my business?

By assessing the importance and urgency of each goal, you can gain clarity on which goals should take precedence over others.

2.3.2 Aligning with Your Vision and Mission

Another crucial aspect of prioritizing your goals is ensuring they align with your vision and mission for your small business. Your vision represents the ultimate destination you want your business to reach, while your mission outlines the purpose and values that guide your business's actions.

Review each goal and assess how well it aligns with your vision and mission. Ask yourself:

- Does this goal contribute to the realization of my business's vision?

- Does it align with the core values and principles that guide my business?

- Will achieving this goal bring me closer to fulfilling my business's mission?

Goals that align closely with your vision and mission should be given higher priority as they are more likely to have a significant impact on your business's overall success and fulfillment of its purpose.

2.3.3 Considering Resources and Constraints

When prioritizing your goals, it's essential to consider the resources and constraints you have available. Resources include your time, finances, skills, and support network, while constraints refer to any limitations or obstacles that may hinder your progress.

Evaluate the resources required to achieve each goal and compare them to the resources you currently have available. Ask yourself:

- Do I have the necessary skills, knowledge, or expertise to pursue this goal?

- Can I allocate the required time and financial resources to achieve this goal?

- Do I have a support network or team that can assist me in accomplishing this goal?

Additionally, consider any constraints or limitations that may impact your ability to pursue certain goals. These constraints could be financial, time-related, or external factors beyond your control. Assess the potential challenges and obstacles associated with each goal and ask yourself:

- Are there any constraints that may hinder my progress toward this goal?

- Can I overcome these constraints or find alternative solutions?

- Are there any goals that may need to be adjusted or postponed due to these constraints?

By considering your available resources and constraints, you can make informed decisions about which goals to prioritize based on feasibility and practicality.

2.3.4 Revisiting and Adjusting Priorities

Prioritizing your goals is not a one-time task. As your business evolves and circumstances change, it's important to regularly revisit and adjust your priorities. This ongoing process ensures that your goals remain aligned with your business's needs and aspirations.

Schedule regular reviews of your goals and assess their progress and relevance. Ask yourself:

- Are there any new goals that have emerged since the last review?

- Have any of the existing goals become more or less important or urgent?

- Are there any goals that need to be deprioritized or replaced with new ones?

By regularly revisiting and adjusting your priorities, you can adapt to changing circumstances and ensure that your efforts are focused on the goals that will have the greatest impact on your small business's success.

Conclusion

Prioritizing your goals is a critical step in the goal mastery process. By assessing the importance and urgency of each goal, aligning them with your vision and mission, considering available resources and constraints, and regularly revisiting and adjusting priorities, you can effectively allocate your time, energy, and resources to achieve the results you have dreamed of for your small business. In the next section, we will explore how to break down your goals into manageable tasks to ensure steady progress toward their achievement.

2.4 Breaking Down Goals into Manageable Tasks

Once you have identified your goals and prioritized them, the next step is to break them down into manageable tasks. Breaking down your goals into smaller tasks not only makes them more achievable but also helps you stay focused and motivated throughout the process. In this section, we will explore the importance of breaking down goals and provide you with practical strategies to effectively manage your tasks.

2.4.1 The Benefits of Breaking Down Goals

Breaking down your goals into manageable tasks offers several benefits that can significantly contribute to your success as a small business owner. Here are some key advantages:

1. Clarity and Focus

When you break down your goals into smaller tasks, you gain clarity on what needs to be done. This clarity allows you to focus on one task at a time, reducing overwhelm and increasing productivity. By having a clear roadmap of tasks, you can stay on track and make progress toward your goals.

2. Motivation and Momentum

Completing smaller tasks gives you a sense of accomplishment and boosts your motivation. As you tick off each task from your list, you build momentum and confidence, propelling you forward toward your larger goals. This positive reinforcement keeps you motivated throughout the journey.

3. Flexibility and Adaptability

Breaking down goals into smaller tasks allows for greater flexibility and adaptability. As circumstances change or new opportunities arise, you can easily adjust your tasks to align with the evolving needs of your business. This flexibility enables you to stay agile and make necessary adjustments without losing sight of your ultimate goals.

4. Efficient Resource Allocation

By breaking down your goals, you can allocate your resources more efficiently. You can identify the specific resources required for each task and allocate them accordingly. This ensures that you make the most of your time, energy, and resources, optimizing your productivity and minimizing waste.

2.4.2 Strategies for Breaking Down Goals

Now that you understand the benefits of breaking down goals, let's explore some strategies to help you effectively manage your tasks:

1. Start with the End in Mind

Before breaking down your goals, visualize the end result you want to achieve. Having a clear vision of the desired outcome will guide you in determining the necessary steps to get there. By starting with the end in mind, you can work backward and break down your goals into smaller, actionable tasks.

2. Identify Milestones

Milestones are significant points of progress toward your goals. Identify key milestones that mark your journey toward success. Breaking down your goals into milestones helps you track your progress and celebrate achievements along the way. These milestones act as checkpoints, keeping you motivated and providing a sense of accomplishment.

3. Prioritize Tasks

Once you have identified your milestones, prioritize the tasks associated with each milestone. Determine which tasks are critical and require immediate attention. Prioritizing tasks ensures that you focus on the most important and impactful activities first, maximizing your productivity and moving you closer to your goals.

4. Break Tasks into Smaller Steps

Take each task and break it down into smaller, manageable steps. This allows you to tackle complex tasks with ease and prevents overwhelm. Breaking tasks into smaller steps also provides a clear roadmap, making it easier to track progress and stay organized.

5. Set Deadlines

Assign deadlines to each task to create a sense of urgency and accountability. Setting deadlines helps you stay focused and ensures that you make consistent progress toward your goals. Be realistic when setting deadlines, considering the complexity and time required for each task.

6. Delegate and Outsource

As a small business owner, you may not have the capacity to handle all tasks on your own. Identify tasks that can be delegated or outsourced to others. Delegating tasks to team members or outsourcing to professionals allows you to focus on high-priority activities while ensuring that all tasks are completed efficiently.

7. Track and Review Progress

Regularly track and review your progress to ensure that you are on track toward your goals. Use project management tools or simple task tracking systems to monitor your tasks and milestones. Regularly reviewing your progress allows you to identify any bottlenecks or areas that require adjustment, keeping you proactive and adaptable.

Conclusion

Breaking down your goals into manageable tasks is a crucial step in achieving small business success. By gaining clarity, staying motivated, and efficiently allocating resources, you can effectively manage your tasks and make consistent progress toward your goals. Use the strategies outlined in this section to break down your goals and create a roadmap for success. Remember, small steps lead to big achievements, so embrace the power of breaking down your goals and watch your dreams become a reality.

3 Removing Your Obstacles

Obstacles can be your biggest enemy or your biggest
ally, wise people can tell the difference.

3.1 Identifying and Overcoming Limiting Beliefs

In order to achieve success in your small business, it is crucial to identify and overcome any limiting beliefs that may be holding you back. Limiting beliefs are negative thoughts or beliefs that we hold about ourselves, our abilities, or the world around us. These beliefs can be deeply ingrained and can have a significant impact on our mindset, motivation, and ultimately, our success.

The Power of Beliefs

Beliefs are powerful. They shape our thoughts, emotions, and actions. If you believe that you are not capable of achieving your goals or that success is only for others, then you are likely to sabotage your own efforts and limit your potential. On the other hand, if you believe in your abilities and have a positive mindset, you are more likely to take action, persevere through challenges, and achieve your desired outcomes.

Identifying Limiting Beliefs

The first step in overcoming limiting beliefs is to identify them. Take some time to reflect on your thoughts and beliefs about yourself, your business, and your goals. Pay attention to any negative or self-defeating thoughts that arise. Common limiting beliefs for small business owners may include:

- "I'm not good enough."

- "I don't have the skills or knowledge to succeed."

- "I don't deserve to be successful."

- "I'm too old/young to achieve my goals."

- "I'm afraid of failure."

- "I don't have enough time/money/resources."

These beliefs can be deeply ingrained and may have been reinforced by past experiences or societal conditioning. However, it is important to remember that beliefs are not facts. They are simply thoughts that we have accepted as true. By challenging and reframing these beliefs, we can begin to overcome them and create a more empowering mindset.

Challenging Limiting Beliefs

Once you have identified your limiting beliefs, it is time to challenge them. Ask yourself the following questions:

1. Is this belief based on facts or is it just a perception?

2. What evidence do I have to support this belief?

3. Are there any counterexamples or instances where this belief has been proven wrong?

4. How is this belief holding me back from achieving my goals?

5. What would be possible if I didn't hold onto this belief?

By questioning the validity of your limiting beliefs, you can start to weaken their hold on you. Look for evidence that contradicts your beliefs and focus on the positive aspects of your abilities and achievements. Surround yourself with positive influences, such as mentors or like-minded individuals, who can help challenge and reshape your beliefs.

Reframing Limiting Beliefs

Once you have challenged your limiting beliefs, it is important to reframe them into more empowering and positive beliefs. For example, if you believe that you are not good enough, reframe it as "I am constantly growing and improving in my skills and abilities." If you believe that you don't have enough time or resources, reframe it as "I am resourceful and can find creative solutions to any challenge."

Reframing your beliefs requires consistent effort and practice. Whenever a negative or limiting thought arises, consciously replace it with a more empowering belief. Use positive affirmations, visualization techniques, and daily reminders to reinforce your new beliefs. Over time, these new beliefs will become ingrained in your mindset and will support your success.

Seeking Support

Overcoming limiting beliefs can be challenging, especially if they have been deeply ingrained over a long period of time. It can be helpful to seek support from a coach, mentor, or therapist who can guide you through the process of identifying and reframing your beliefs. They can provide valuable insights, tools, and techniques to help you overcome your limiting beliefs and achieve your goals.

Remember, your beliefs shape your reality. By identifying and overcoming limiting beliefs, you can create a mindset that is aligned with your goals and aspirations. Embrace the power of positive thinking and empower yourself to achieve the success you have always dreamed of.

3.2 Dealing with Procrastination and Time Management

Procrastination and poor time management are common challenges that many small business owners face. These issues can hinder productivity and prevent you from achieving your goals. In this section, we will explore strategies to overcome procrastination and improve time management skills, allowing you to make the most of your time and achieve success in your business.

Understanding Procrastination

Procrastination is the act of delaying or postponing tasks or actions that need to be completed. It is often driven by a desire to avoid discomfort or fear of failure. As a small business owner, it is crucial to recognize the negative impact that procrastination can have on your business. It can lead to missed opportunities, decreased productivity, and increased stress levels.

Identifying the Causes of Procrastination

To effectively deal with procrastination, it is essential to identify the underlying causes. Some common causes of procrastination include:

Lack of Clarity

When you are unsure about the specific steps required to achieve your goals, it can be challenging to take action. Lack of clarity can lead to indecision and procrastination. To overcome this, ensure that your goals are well-defined and break them down into smaller, manageable tasks.

Fear of Failure

Fear of failure can paralyze you and prevent you from taking action. It is important to recognize that failure is a natural part of the learning process and an opportunity for growth. Embrace a growth mindset and view failures as valuable lessons that can propel you forward.

Overwhelm

Feeling overwhelmed by the sheer number of tasks and responsibilities can lead to procrastination. It is crucial to prioritize your tasks and focus on the most important ones. Break down larger tasks into smaller, more manageable steps to make them less overwhelming.

Perfectionism

Perfectionism can be a significant barrier to productivity. Striving for perfection can lead to excessive time spent on minor details and unnecessary delays. Embrace the concept of "good enough" and prioritize progress over perfection.

Strategies for Overcoming Procrastination

Now that we have identified some common causes of procrastination let's explore strategies to overcome it and improve time management skills:

Set Clear and Specific Goals

Setting clear and specific goals provides a sense of direction and purpose. When you have a clear vision of what you want to achieve, it becomes easier to prioritize tasks and take action. Break down your goals into smaller, actionable steps, and set deadlines for each task.

Create a Schedule and Stick to It

Developing a schedule and sticking to it is crucial for effective time management. Allocate specific time slots for different tasks and activities, including breaks and downtime. Use tools such as calendars or productivity apps to help you stay organized and on track.

Prioritize Tasks

Not all tasks are created equal. Prioritize your tasks based on their importance and urgency. Focus on high-priority tasks that align with your goals and have the most significant impact on your business. Delegate or eliminate tasks that are not essential.

Break Tasks into Manageable Chunks

Large tasks can be overwhelming and lead to procrastination. Break them down into smaller, more manageable chunks. This approach allows you to make progress and build momentum, increasing your motivation to continue working.

Use Time-Blocking Techniques

Time-blocking is a technique that involves assigning specific time blocks for different tasks or activities. This method helps you allocate dedicated time for each task, minimizing distractions and increasing focus. Experiment with different time-blocking techniques to find what works best for you.

Minimize Distractions

Distractions can significantly impact your productivity. Identify common distractions in your work environment and take steps to minimize them. This may include turning off notifications on your phone, closing unnecessary tabs on your computer, or finding a quiet workspace.

Practice the Pomodoro Technique

The Pomodoro Technique is a time management method that involves working in focused bursts, typically 25 minutes, followed by short breaks. This technique helps improve focus and productivity by breaking work into manageable intervals. Set a timer for each work session and take short breaks in between.

Develop Self-Discipline

Self-discipline is crucial for overcoming procrastination and managing your time effectively. Set clear boundaries and hold yourself accountable for sticking to your schedule and completing tasks. Develop habits and routines that support your productivity and eliminate distractions.

Seek Accountability and Support

Accountability can be a powerful motivator. Share your goals and progress with a trusted friend, mentor, or business coach who can hold you accountable. Joining a mastermind group or finding an accountability partner can also provide support and encouragement.

Conclusion

Procrastination and poor time management can hinder your progress as a small business owner. By understanding the causes of procrastination and implementing effective strategies, you can overcome these challenges and improve your productivity. Set clear goals, create a schedule, prioritize tasks, and develop self-discipline. Remember, success is not achieved overnight, but with consistent effort and a proactive approach to time management, you can achieve your goals and create the business of your dreams.

3.3 Managing Stress and Overcoming Fear

Managing stress and overcoming fear are crucial aspects of achieving small business success. As a small business owner, you are likely to face numerous challenges and uncertainties that can lead to stress and fear. However, by implementing effective strategies to manage stress and overcome fear, you can maintain a positive mindset and navigate through difficult situations with confidence.

3.3.1 Understanding Stress and Fear

Before diving into strategies to manage stress and overcome fear, it is important to understand the nature of these emotions and their impact on your business. Stress is a natural response to demanding situations, and while a certain level of stress can be motivating, excessive stress can hinder your productivity and decision-making abilities. Fear, on the other hand, is an emotional response to perceived threats or risks, which can prevent you from taking necessary risks and seizing opportunities.

3.3.2 Identifying Sources of Stress and Fear

To effectively manage stress and overcome fear, it is essential to identify the sources that trigger these emotions. Common sources of stress for small business owners include financial pressures, time constraints, competition, and the responsibility of managing employees. Fear can arise from the fear of failure, fear of rejection, fear of making wrong decisions, or fear of stepping out of your comfort zone. By identifying the specific sources of stress and fear in your business, you can develop targeted strategies to address them.

3.3.3 Developing Stress Management Techniques

Stress management techniques are essential tools for small business owners to maintain their well-being and productivity. Here are some effective strategies to manage stress:

1. **Time Management**: Implementing effective time management techniques can help you prioritize tasks, set realistic deadlines, and avoid feeling overwhelmed. Use tools such as to-do lists, calendars, and project management software to stay organized and manage your time efficiently.

2. **Self-Care**: Taking care of your physical and mental well-being is crucial for managing stress. Make sure to prioritize activities such as exercise, proper nutrition, sufficient sleep, and relaxation techniques like meditation or deep breathing exercises. Taking breaks throughout the day can also help you recharge and reduce stress levels.

3. **Delegate and Outsource**: As a small business owner, it can be tempting to take on all tasks yourself. However, delegat-

ing and outsourcing tasks that are not within your expertise or that can be handled by others can alleviate stress and free up your time to focus on more important aspects of your business.

4. **Seek Support**: Surround yourself with a supportive network of mentors, peers, or business coaches who can provide guidance, advice, and emotional support. Sharing your challenges and concerns with others who understand the entrepreneurial journey can help alleviate stress and provide fresh perspectives.

5. **Practice Mindfulness**: Mindfulness is the practice of being fully present in the moment and non-judgmentally aware of your thoughts and emotions. Incorporating mindfulness techniques into your daily routine, such as mindfulness meditation or mindful breathing exercises, can help reduce stress and increase your ability to handle challenging situations.

3.3.4 Overcoming Fear and Taking Calculated Risks

Fear can be a significant barrier to small business success, as it often prevents entrepreneurs from taking necessary risks and pursuing growth opportunities. Here are some strategies to overcome fear and embrace calculated risks:

1. **Challenge Negative Thoughts**: Fear often stems from negative thoughts and self-doubt. Challenge these thoughts by questioning their validity and replacing them with positive affirmations. Remind yourself of your past successes and

focus on the potential positive outcomes of taking risks.

2. **Take Small Steps**: Overcoming fear does not mean diving headfirst into the unknown. Start by taking small steps outside of your comfort zone and gradually increase the level of risk. Each small success will build your confidence and make it easier to tackle bigger challenges.

3. **Visualize Success**: Visualization is a powerful technique that can help overcome fear by mentally rehearsing successful outcomes. Take time to visualize yourself achieving your goals and facing challenges with confidence. This practice can help rewire your brain to associate positive emotions with taking risks.

4. **Seek Knowledge and Expertise**: Fear often arises from a lack of knowledge or expertise in a particular area. Invest in your personal and professional development by attending workshops, seminars, or enrolling in courses to gain the necessary skills and knowledge. Surround yourself with experts who can provide guidance and support.

5. **Celebrate Progress**: Celebrate your achievements, no matter how small. Recognize and reward yourself for taking risks and stepping outside of your comfort zone. This positive reinforcement will help build your confidence and motivate you to continue pushing past fear.

By implementing these strategies, you can effectively manage stress and overcome fear, allowing you to operate your small business with clarity, confidence, and resilience. Remember, managing stress and overcoming fear is an ongoing process, and it requires consistent effort and self-reflection. Embrace the challenges and uncertainties that come with entrepreneurship, and use them as opportunities for personal and professional growth.

3.4 Building a Supportive Network

Building a supportive network is a crucial aspect of achieving success in any endeavor, especially in the world of small business. As a small business owner, you may often find yourself facing challenges and obstacles that can be overwhelming to tackle alone. That's where a supportive network comes in. By surrounding yourself with like-minded individuals who share your goals and aspirations, you can gain valuable insights, support, and encouragement to help you navigate the ups and downs of entrepreneurship.

3.4.1 The Power of Networking

Networking is the process of establishing and nurturing relationships with individuals who can provide support, guidance, and resources to help you achieve your goals. It involves connecting with people from various backgrounds, industries, and expertise levels to exchange ideas, knowledge, and opportunities. Networking is not just about making connections; it's about building meaningful relationships based on trust, mutual respect, and shared interests.

Networking can take many forms, from attending industry conferences and events to joining professional associations and online communities. The key is to be proactive and intentional in seeking out opportunities to connect with others who can contribute to your growth and success.

3.4.2 Identifying Your Network

When building a supportive network, it's important to identify the types of individuals who can provide the most value to your small business. Start by considering your specific goals and the areas in which you need support. For example, if you're looking to expand your customer base, connecting with marketing professionals or other business owners who have successfully grown their customer base can be beneficial.

Additionally, consider the diversity of your network. Surrounding yourself with individuals from different industries, backgrounds, and perspectives can provide fresh insights and ideas that you may not have considered otherwise. Don't limit yourself to individuals who are similar to you; embrace diversity and seek out connections that can challenge and inspire you.

3.4.3 Building Relationships

Building relationships within your network requires time, effort, and genuine interest in others. It's not just about what others can do for you; it's about how you can contribute to their success as well. Here are some strategies to help you build strong and meaningful relationships within your network:

1. Be proactive: Take the initiative to reach out to individuals who you believe can contribute to your goals. Attend networking events, join online communities, and participate in industry forums to connect with like-minded individuals.

2. Listen actively: When engaging in conversations with others, listen attentively and show genuine interest in what they

have to say. Ask open-ended questions and seek to understand their perspectives and experiences.

3. Offer support: Be willing to offer your support, knowledge, and resources to others within your network. By being generous with your time and expertise, you can build trust and establish yourself as a valuable resource.

4. Follow up: After connecting with someone, make sure to follow up and maintain regular communication. This can be through email, phone calls, or in-person meetings. Stay engaged and show that you value the relationship.

5. Be authentic: Be yourself and let your true personality shine through. Authenticity is key to building genuine connections that can withstand the test of time.

3.4.4 Leveraging Your Network

Once you have established a supportive network, it's important to leverage it effectively to maximize its benefits. Here are some ways you can leverage your network to support your small business:

1. Seek advice and guidance: When faced with challenges or difficult decisions, reach out to individuals within your network who have relevant expertise or experience. Their insights and advice can help you make informed decisions and overcome obstacles.

2. Collaborate and partner: Look for opportunities to collaborate with other businesses or professionals within your network. By combining your strengths and resources, you

can create mutually beneficial partnerships that can lead to growth and success.

3. Share knowledge and resources: Be willing to share your knowledge, insights, and resources with others within your network. This not only strengthens your relationships but also positions you as a valuable and trusted member of the community.

4. Celebrate successes: When members of your network achieve success, celebrate their accomplishments and show your support. This not only fosters a positive and supportive environment but also strengthens the bonds within your network.

5. Stay connected: Regularly engage with individuals within your network to stay updated on their progress and to maintain the relationship. This can be through social media, email newsletters, or in-person meetings.

3.4.5 Expanding Your Network

Building a supportive network is an ongoing process. As your goals and needs evolve, it's important to continuously expand and diversify your network. Here are some strategies to help you expand your network:

1. Attend industry events: Participate in conferences, seminars, and trade shows related to your industry. These events provide excellent opportunities to meet new people and establish connections.

2. Join professional associations: Become a member of professional associations and organizations relevant to your industry. These associations often host networking events and provide resources and support for their members.

3. Engage in online communities: Join online communities, forums, and social media groups related to your industry. Engaging in discussions and sharing your expertise can help you connect with like-minded individuals from around the world.

4. Seek mentorship: Find mentors who can provide guidance, support, and advice based on their own experiences. Mentors can be invaluable in helping you navigate the challenges of entrepreneurship and achieve your goals.

5. Give back: Actively contribute to your network by offering your support, knowledge, and resources to others. By being a valuable and generous member of the community, you will attract like-minded individuals who can contribute to your growth and success.

Building a supportive network is not just about finding people who can help you achieve your goals; it's about creating a community of individuals who share your values, aspirations, and commitment to success. By investing time and effort into building and nurturing relationships within your network, you can create a support system that will propel you toward your dreams and aspirations.

4 Enhancing Your Strategies

Great journeys begin with single steps, and consistent
steps build bridges to where our journey leads

4.1 Developing Effective Planning and Organization Skills

E ffective planning and organization skills are essential for small
business owners who want to achieve their goals and maximize
their productivity. Without proper planning and organization, it can
be challenging to stay focused, meet deadlines, and make progress toward your desired outcomes. In this section, we will explore strategies
and techniques to help you develop and enhance your planning and
organization skills.

4.1.1 Setting Clear Objectives

Before you can effectively plan and organize your tasks and activities, it is crucial to have clear objectives in mind. Objectives provide direction and purpose, helping you prioritize your efforts and allocate resources effectively. When setting objectives, it is essential to make them specific, measurable, achievable, relevant, and time-bound (SMART). By following the SMART framework, you can ensure that your objectives are well-defined and actionable.

To set clear objectives, start by identifying what you want to achieve. Break down your long-term goals into smaller, more manageable milestones. Each milestone should have a specific outcome and a deadline for completion. By setting clear objectives, you can create a roadmap for your business and stay focused on what needs to be done.

4.1.2 Creating a Strategic Plan

Once you have set clear objectives, the next step is to create a strategic plan. A strategic plan outlines the actions and steps you need to take to achieve your objectives. It helps you identify the resources, timelines, and milestones required to reach your goals.

When creating a strategic plan, consider the following:

1. Identify the key activities and tasks required to achieve each objective.

2. Determine the resources, such as finances, personnel, and technology, needed to support your plan.

3. Establish timelines and deadlines for each task and milestone.

4. Assign responsibilities to team members or yourself to ensure accountability.

5. Regularly review and update your strategic plan to adapt to changing circumstances.

By creating a strategic plan, you can effectively allocate your time and resources, ensuring that you are working toward your objectives in a structured and organized manner.

4.1.3 Prioritizing Tasks and Activities

As a small business owner, you likely have a multitude of tasks and activities competing for your attention. To stay organized and productive, it is crucial to prioritize your tasks effectively. Prioritization involves identifying the most important and urgent tasks and allocating your time and resources accordingly.

To prioritize tasks, consider the following:

1. Identify tasks that directly contribute to your objectives and focus on those first.

2. Evaluate the urgency of each task and determine which ones require immediate attention.

3. Consider the potential impact of each task on your business's overall success.

4. Break down larger tasks into smaller, more manageable subtasks.

5. Use tools such as to-do lists, project management software, or time management apps to help you stay organized.

By prioritizing tasks, you can ensure that you are focusing your efforts on activities that will have the most significant impact on your business's success.

4.1.4 Time Management Techniques

Effective time management is a crucial skill for small business owners. It involves managing your time efficiently to accomplish tasks and meet deadlines. By implementing time management techniques, you can increase your productivity and reduce stress.

Here are some time management techniques to consider:

1. Prioritize tasks and allocate specific time blocks for each task.

2. Use a calendar or scheduling tool to plan your day, week, or month in advance.

3. Break larger tasks into smaller, more manageable chunks.

4. Avoid multitasking and focus on one task at a time.

5. Minimize distractions by turning off notifications or setting specific times for checking emails and messages.

6. Delegate tasks that can be handled by others, freeing up your time for more critical activities.

7. Take regular breaks to recharge and maintain focus.

By implementing effective time management techniques, you can make the most of your available time and accomplish more in less time.

4.1.5 Utilizing Technology and Tools

In today's digital age, there are numerous technology and tools available to help small business owners with planning and organization. These tools can streamline processes, automate tasks, and improve overall efficiency.

Consider utilizing the following technology and tools:

1. Project management software: Helps you track tasks, deadlines, and progress.

2. Collaboration tools: Facilitate communication and collaboration among team members.

3. Time tracking software: Allows you to monitor how you spend your time and identify areas for improvement.

4. Cloud storage solutions: Enable easy access to files and documents from anywhere.

5. Task management apps: Help you stay organized and manage your to-do lists effectively.

By leveraging technology and tools, you can enhance your planning and organization skills, streamline processes, and improve overall productivity.

4.1.6 Reviewing and Adjusting Your Plans

Effective planning and organization skills require regular review and adjustment. As your business evolves and circumstances change, it is essential to review your plans and make necessary adjustments to stay on track.

Regularly review your plans by:

1. Assessing progress toward your objectives.

2. Identifying any obstacles or challenges that may be hindering your progress.

3. Evaluating the effectiveness of your strategies and adjusting them as needed.

4. Seeking feedback from team members or mentors to gain different perspectives.

By regularly reviewing and adjusting your plans, you can ensure that you are staying aligned with your goals and making the necessary changes to achieve success.

In conclusion, developing effective planning and organization skills is crucial for small business owners who want to maximize their productivity and achieve their goals. By setting clear objectives, creating strategic plans, prioritizing tasks, implementing time management techniques, utilizing technology and tools, and regularly reviewing and adjusting your plans, you can enhance your planning and organization skills and increase your chances of success. Remember, effective planning and organization are the foundation for turning your dreams into reality.

4.2 Improving Decision-Making and Problem-Solving

As a small business owner, you are faced with countless decisions and problems on a daily basis. The ability to make effective decisions and solve problems efficiently is crucial for the success of your business. In this section, we will explore strategies and techniques to improve your decision-making and problem-solving skills.

4.2.1 The Importance of Decision-Making

Decision-making is an integral part of running a small business. Every decision you make has the potential to impact your business's growth, profitability, and overall success. It is essential to approach decision-making with a clear and rational mindset.

Analyzing the Situation

Before making any decision, it is important to thoroughly analyze the situation. Gather all the relevant information and consider the potential outcomes and consequences of each option. This will help you make an informed decision based on facts rather than emotions or assumptions.

Evaluating Options

Once you have analyzed the situation, it is time to evaluate the available options. Consider the pros and cons of each option and assess how they align with your business goals and values. Prioritize the options based on their potential impact and feasibility.

Making the Decision

After evaluating the options, it is time to make a decision. Trust your instincts, but also rely on the information and analysis you have conducted. Remember that not making a decision is also a decision in itself, so avoid analysis paralysis and take action.

4.2.2 Problem-Solving Techniques

Problem-solving is a skill that can be developed and honed over time. By utilizing effective problem-solving techniques, you can overcome challenges and find innovative solutions for your business.

Define the Problem

The first step in problem-solving is to clearly define the problem. Identify the root cause and understand the impact it has on your business. By defining the problem, you can focus your efforts on finding a solution that addresses the underlying issue.

Brainstorming

Once the problem is defined, it is time to brainstorm potential solutions. Encourage creativity and open-mindedness during this process. Consider involving your team members or seeking input from external sources to gather diverse perspectives and ideas.

Evaluate and Select the Best Solution

After generating a list of potential solutions, evaluate each option based on its feasibility, effectiveness, and alignment with your business goals. Consider the resources required, potential risks, and long-term implications. Select the solution that best addresses the problem while considering the overall impact on your business.

Implement and Monitor

Once you have selected a solution, it is time to implement it. Develop an action plan and allocate the necessary resources to execute the solution effectively. Monitor the progress and make adjustments as needed. Regularly evaluate the effectiveness of the solution and make improvements if necessary.

4.2.3 Decision-Making and Problem-Solving in a Team

In a small business, decision-making and problem-solving often involve collaboration with your team members. It is important to foster a culture of open communication and encourage team members to contribute their ideas and perspectives.

Effective Communication

Clear and effective communication is essential for successful decision-making and problem-solving in a team. Encourage open dialogue and active listening among team members. Ensure that everyone has the opportunity to express their opinions and ideas.

Collaboration and Consensus

When making decisions as a team, strive for consensus whenever possible. Collaboration allows for a more comprehensive analysis of the situation and increases the likelihood of finding the best solution. However, it is important to balance collaboration with efficiency and avoid getting stuck in endless discussions.

Delegating Responsibility

In problem-solving, it is important to delegate responsibility to team members who have the necessary skills and expertise. By involving others in the process, you can leverage their strengths and increase the chances of finding innovative solutions.

Learning from Mistakes

Not every decision or problem-solving attempt will yield the desired results. It is important to view mistakes as learning opportunities and encourage a culture of continuous improvement. Analyze what went wrong, identify the lessons learned, and apply them to future decision-making and problem-solving processes.

4.2.4 Tools and Techniques for Decision-Making and Problem-Solving

There are various tools and techniques available to assist you in making effective decisions and solving complex problems. Here are a few commonly used ones:

SWOT Analysis

SWOT (Strengths, Weaknesses, Opportunities, and Threats) analysis is a framework that helps you evaluate the internal and external factors that can impact your business. By identifying your strengths and weaknesses, as well as the opportunities and threats in your industry, you can make more informed decisions.

Decision Matrix

A decision matrix is a tool that allows you to evaluate multiple options based on different criteria. By assigning weights to each criterion and scoring each option, you can objectively compare and prioritize the options.

Root Cause Analysis

Root cause analysis is a technique used to identify the underlying cause of a problem. By digging deeper into the problem and understanding its root cause, you can develop more effective solutions that address the core issue.

Six Thinking Hats

The Six Thinking Hats technique, developed by Edward de Bono, is a method for exploring different perspectives during problem-solving. Each "hat" represents a different thinking style, such as logical, emotional, creative, and critical thinking. By considering each perspective, you can generate a more comprehensive understanding of the problem and potential solutions.

In conclusion, improving your decision-making and problem-solving skills is essential for the success of your small business. By approaching decisions with a rational mindset, utilizing effective problem-solving techniques, fostering collaboration within your team, and utilizing tools and techniques, you can make informed decisions and find innovative solutions to overcome challenges. Remember, decision-making and problem-solving are skills that can be developed and refined over time, so embrace continuous learning and improvement.

4.3 Utilizing Effective Communication and Negotiation

Effective communication and negotiation are essential skills for small business owners who want to achieve their goals and succeed in their endeavors. In this section, we will explore the importance of effective communication and negotiation in the context of the DREAM Method and provide practical strategies to enhance these skills.

4.3.1 The Power of Effective Communication

Communication is the foundation of any successful business. It is the key to building strong relationships with customers, employees, suppliers, and other stakeholders. Effective communication allows you to convey your ideas, goals, and expectations clearly, ensuring that everyone is on the same page and working toward a common objective.

Active Listening

One of the most important aspects of effective communication is active listening. When you actively listen to others, you demonstrate respect and empathy, which helps to build trust and rapport. Active listening involves giving your full attention to the speaker, maintaining eye contact, and asking clarifying questions to ensure that you understand their message accurately.

Clear and Concise Communication

Clear and concise communication is crucial in avoiding misunderstandings and confusion. When communicating with others, whether it's through written or verbal means, strive to be clear and concise in your message. Use simple and straightforward language, avoid jargon or technical terms that may be unfamiliar to others, and provide specific details and examples to illustrate your point.

Non-Verbal Communication

Non-verbal communication plays a significant role in conveying your message effectively. Your body language, facial expressions, and tone of voice can all influence how your message is received. Be mindful of your non-verbal cues and ensure that they align with your intended message. Maintain an open and approachable posture, make eye contact, and use appropriate gestures to enhance your communication.

4.3.2 The Art of Negotiation

Negotiation is a skill that every small business owner should master. Whether you are negotiating with suppliers, clients, or employees, the ability to find mutually beneficial solutions is essential for long-term success. Here are some strategies to enhance your negotiation skills:

Preparation

Before entering into any negotiation, it is crucial to be well-prepared. Research and gather information about the other party's needs, interests, and alternatives. Identify your own goals and priorities, and determine your walk-away point. By being prepared, you will feel more confident and be better equipped to navigate the negotiation process.

Active Listening and Empathy

Just as in effective communication, active listening is also vital in negotiation. By actively listening to the other party's needs and concerns, you can better understand their perspective and find common ground. Show empathy and try to put yourself in their shoes to build rapport and trust.

Win-Win Solutions

Strive for win-win solutions in negotiations. Look for opportunities to create value for both parties involved. Instead of focusing solely on your own interests, explore ways to meet the other party's needs while still achieving your goals. This collaborative approach fosters positive relationships and sets the foundation for future cooperation.

Flexibility and Creativity

Negotiation often requires flexibility and creativity to find innovative solutions. Be open to alternative proposals and consider different options that may not have been initially apparent. By thinking outside the box, you can uncover opportunities that benefit both parties and lead to successful outcomes.

Effective Communication

Effective communication is crucial during the negotiation process. Clearly articulate your needs, interests, and expectations, and actively listen to the other party's perspective. Use clear and concise language, ask clarifying questions, and seek to understand before being understood. By maintaining open and honest communication, you can build trust and foster a positive negotiation environment.

4.3.3 Overcoming Communication and Negotiation Challenges

Communication and negotiation can sometimes be challenging, especially in high-stakes situations. Here are some common challenges and strategies to overcome them:

Emotional Intelligence

Emotional intelligence is the ability to recognize and manage your own emotions and those of others. It plays a significant role in effective communication and negotiation. Develop your emotional intelligence by practicing self-awareness, empathy, and emotional regulation. By understanding and managing emotions, you can navigate challenging situations more effectively.

Conflict Resolution

Conflicts may arise during communication and negotiation. It is essential to address conflicts promptly and constructively. Use active listening and empathy to understand the underlying issues, and seek common ground for resolution. Consider involving a neutral third party, such as a mediator, if necessary, to facilitate the resolution process.

Building Relationships

Building strong relationships is crucial for effective communication and negotiation. Invest time and effort in building rapport and trust with your stakeholders. Show genuine interest in their needs and concerns, and follow through on your commitments. By nurturing relationships, you create a foundation of trust that can support successful communication and negotiation.

Continuous Improvement

Communication and negotiation skills can always be improved. Seek feedback from others, reflect on your own performance, and identify areas for growth. Invest in professional development opportunities, such as workshops or courses, to enhance your skills further. By continuously improving your communication and negotiation abilities, you can become a more effective small business owner.

In conclusion, effective communication and negotiation are essential skills for small business owners. By mastering these skills, you can build strong relationships, resolve conflicts, and achieve mutually beneficial outcomes. Utilize the strategies outlined in this section to enhance your communication and negotiation abilities and propel your business toward success.

4.4 Adapting to Change and Embracing Innovation

In today's fast-paced and ever-changing business landscape, the ability to adapt to change and embrace innovation is crucial for small business owners. The world is constantly evolving, and businesses that fail to keep up with the latest trends and technologies risk being left behind. In this section, we will explore the importance of adapting to change and how embracing innovation can propel your small business to new heights.

4.4.1 Embracing a Growth Mindset

One of the key factors in adapting to change and embracing innovation is having a growth mindset. A growth mindset is the belief that your abilities and intelligence can be developed through dedication and hard work. It is about viewing challenges as opportunities for growth and learning, rather than as obstacles.

As a small business owner, it is essential to cultivate a growth mindset not only within yourself but also within your team. Encourage your employees to embrace change and see it as an opportunity for personal and professional development. Foster a culture of continuous learning and improvement, where everyone is encouraged to think outside the box and explore new ideas.

4.4.2 Staying Agile and Flexible

Adapting to change requires agility and flexibility. As a small business owner, you need to be able to quickly respond to market trends, customer demands, and industry shifts. This means being open to new ideas, being willing to pivot your business strategy when necessary, and being able to make decisions on the fly.

To stay agile and flexible, it is important to regularly assess your business processes and strategies. Keep an eye on industry trends and competitor activities. Stay connected with your customers and listen to their feedback. By staying informed and being proactive, you can identify opportunities for innovation and make the necessary adjustments to stay ahead of the curve.

4.4.3 Embracing Innovation

Innovation is the lifeblood of any successful business. It is about finding new and better ways of doing things, whether it's developing new products or services, improving existing processes, or finding creative solutions to customer problems. Embracing innovation allows you to stay competitive, attract new customers, and differentiate yourself from your competitors.

To foster a culture of innovation within your small business, encourage your team to think creatively and challenge the status quo. Create an environment where ideas are welcomed and rewarded. Implement regular brainstorming sessions or innovation workshops to generate new ideas and solutions. Embrace technology and explore how it can streamline your business processes and improve efficiency.

4.4.4 Embracing Change

Change can be intimidating, especially for small business owners who have invested time and resources into their current strategies and processes. However, resisting change can be detrimental to your business's long-term success. Embracing change allows you to stay relevant, adapt to new market conditions, and seize new opportunities.

To embrace change effectively, it is important to communicate openly with your team. Explain the reasons behind the change and how it aligns with your business goals. Involve your employees in the decision-making process and provide them with the necessary support and resources to navigate the transition. Celebrate small wins along the way to keep morale high and maintain momentum.

4.4.5 Collaborating and Networking

Collaboration and networking are essential for small business owners looking to adapt to change and embrace innovation. By collaborating with other businesses, you can leverage each other's strengths and resources, share knowledge and expertise, and explore new opportunities together.

Networking is also crucial for staying connected with industry trends and finding potential partners or mentors. Attend industry conferences, join professional associations, and participate in online communities to expand your network and stay informed about the latest developments in your industry.

4.4.6 Embracing Failure as a Learning Opportunity

Innovation and change often come with risks, and failure is a natural part of the process. Instead of fearing failure, embrace it as a learning opportunity. When things don't go as planned, take the time to analyze what went wrong and identify areas for improvement. Encourage your team to share their failures and learnings, creating a culture of continuous improvement and resilience.

By adapting to change and embracing innovation, you position your small business for long-term success. It allows you to stay ahead of the competition, meet the evolving needs of your customers, and seize new opportunities as they arise. Embrace change, foster a culture of innovation, and cultivate a growth mindset within yourself and your team. With the DREAM Method as your guide, you can navigate the ever-changing business landscape and achieve the success you have always dreamed of.

5 Automating Your Systems

Consistent strategies build sustainable systems that
can withstand the journey of many travelers.

5.1 Streamlining Business Processes

S treamlining business processes is a crucial aspect of small business success. By optimizing and automating your systems, you can increase efficiency, reduce costs, and improve overall productivity. In this section, we will explore various strategies and techniques to help you streamline your business processes effectively.

5.1.1 Assessing Your Current Processes

Before you can streamline your business processes, it is essential to assess your current workflows and identify areas that need improvement. Take the time to evaluate each step of your processes and determine if there are any bottlenecks, redundancies, or inefficiencies. This assessment will provide you with valuable insights into where you can make changes to optimize your operations.

5.1.2 Mapping Out Your Ideal Processes

Once you have assessed your current processes, the next step is to map out your ideal processes. This involves envisioning how you would like your workflows to function ideally. Consider the most efficient and effective way to complete each task and identify any opportunities for automation or simplification. By mapping out your ideal processes, you can create a clear roadmap for streamlining your operations.

5.1.3 Implementing Process Automation

Process automation is a powerful tool for streamlining business processes. By automating repetitive and time-consuming tasks, you can free up valuable time and resources to focus on more critical aspects of your business. There are various automation tools and software available that can help you automate tasks such as data entry, email marketing, inventory management, and customer support. Evaluate your business needs and explore automation solutions that align with your goals.

5.1.4 Integrating Technology Solutions

In today's digital age, technology plays a vital role in streamlining business processes. Look for technology solutions that can integrate seamlessly with your existing systems and enhance your operations. For example, implementing a customer relationship management (CRM) system can centralize customer data, improve communication, and streamline sales processes. Similarly, project management tools can help you track and manage tasks more efficiently. Embrace technology and leverage it to optimize your business processes.

5.1.5 Outsourcing and Delegating Tasks

Outsourcing and delegating tasks can be a game-changer when it comes to streamlining your business processes. Identify tasks that can be outsourced to external professionals or delegated to capable team members. This allows you to focus on your core competencies while ensuring that all necessary tasks are completed efficiently. When outsourcing, be sure to choose reliable and reputable service providers who align with your business values and goals.

5.1.6 Creating Standard Operating Procedures (SOPs)

Standard Operating Procedures (SOPs) are essential documents that outline step-by-step instructions for completing specific tasks or processes. By creating SOPs, you can ensure consistency and efficiency in your operations. Document each process in detail, including the necessary tools, resources, and timelines. SOPs not only streamline your business processes but also serve as valuable training materials for new employees.

5.1.7 Continuously Monitoring and Improving Processes

Streamlining business processes is an ongoing effort. It is crucial to continuously monitor and evaluate your streamlined processes to identify any areas that may need further improvement. Regularly review your SOPs, gather feedback from your team, and stay updated on the latest industry trends and best practices. By embracing a culture of continuous improvement, you can ensure that your business processes remain optimized and efficient.

5.1.8 Embracing a Lean Mindset

A lean mindset is all about eliminating waste and maximizing value. Embrace the principles of lean management, such as identifying and eliminating non-value-added activities, reducing unnecessary steps, and optimizing resource allocation. By adopting a lean mindset, you can streamline your business processes and create a more efficient and productive work environment.

5.1.9 Training and Empowering Your Team

Streamlining business processes is not just about implementing new tools and technologies; it also involves training and empowering your team. Provide your employees with the necessary training and resources to understand and execute the streamlined processes effectively. Encourage open communication, collaboration, and innovation within your team. When your team is well-trained and empowered, they can contribute to the continuous improvement of your business processes.

5.1.10 Measuring and Tracking Key Performance Indicators (KPIs)

To ensure the effectiveness of your streamlined processes, it is essential to measure and track key performance indicators (KPIs). Identify the metrics that align with your business goals and regularly monitor them to gauge the success of your streamlined processes. KPIs can include metrics such as productivity, customer satisfaction, cost savings, and cycle time. Use these metrics to make data-driven decisions and identify areas for further improvement.

By streamlining your business processes, you can optimize your operations, increase productivity, and ultimately achieve your small business goals. Embrace the strategies and techniques discussed in this section to create efficient workflows that drive success. Remember, continuous improvement and adaptation are key to maintaining streamlined processes in an ever-evolving business landscape.

5.2 Implementing Technology and Software Solutions

In today's fast-paced and technologically advanced world, implementing technology and software solutions is crucial for small business success. Technology has revolutionized the way we do business, making tasks more efficient, improving communication, and streamlining processes. By embracing technology and utilizing software solutions, small business owners can gain a competitive edge, increase productivity, and achieve their goals more effectively.

5.2.1 Assessing Your Technological Needs

Before implementing any technology or software solutions, it is essential to assess your business's specific technological needs. This involves evaluating your current processes, identifying areas that can be improved, and determining which technologies and software will best meet those needs. Consider factors such as the size of your business, the nature of your industry, and the goals you want to achieve.

Start by conducting a thorough analysis of your existing systems and processes. Identify any bottlenecks, inefficiencies, or areas where manual tasks can be automated. This analysis will help you understand which technologies and software solutions will be most beneficial for your business.

5.2.2 Researching and Selecting the Right Technology and Software Solutions

Once you have assessed your technological needs, it's time to research and select the right technology and software solutions for your business. There are numerous options available, ranging from project management tools and customer relationship management (CRM) software to accounting software and communication platforms.

Start by researching different software providers and technologies that align with your business needs. Consider factors such as functionality, ease of use, scalability, and cost. Read reviews, compare features, and seek recommendations from other small business owners or industry experts. It's important to choose solutions that are user-friendly, reliable, and compatible with your existing systems.

When selecting technology and software solutions, keep in mind the specific goals you want to achieve. For example, if you aim to improve customer relationship management, consider CRM software that offers robust features for tracking customer interactions, managing leads, and analyzing data. If you want to streamline your accounting processes, look for accounting software that integrates with your bank accounts and offers features like invoicing, expense tracking, and financial reporting.

5.2.3 Implementing and Integrating Technology and Software Solutions

Once you have selected the technology and software solutions that best fit your business needs, it's time to implement and integrate them into your existing systems. This process may involve several steps, depending on the complexity of the solutions you have chosen.

Start by creating a detailed implementation plan. This plan should outline the steps required to install, configure, and integrate the technology and software solutions. Assign responsibilities to team members, set deadlines, and establish a timeline for the implementation process. It's crucial to communicate the plan to all relevant stakeholders and ensure everyone understands their roles and responsibilities.

During the implementation process, it's important to provide adequate training and support to your team members. Conduct training sessions to familiarize them with the new technology and software solutions and ensure they understand how to use them effectively. Offer ongoing support and address any questions or concerns that arise during the transition period.

Integrating technology and software solutions with your existing systems is also crucial for maximizing their effectiveness. Ensure that the new solutions seamlessly integrate with your current processes and workflows. This may involve customizing settings, importing data, or establishing connections with other software or platforms. Test the integration thoroughly to ensure everything is functioning as expected before fully adopting the new solutions.

5.2.4 Monitoring and Evaluating the Impact of Technology and Software Solutions

After implementing technology and software solutions, it's important to monitor and evaluate their impact on your business. Regularly assess whether the solutions are delivering the expected benefits and helping you achieve your goals. This evaluation process will help you identify any areas for improvement and make necessary adjustments.

Monitor key performance indicators (KPIs) to track the effectiveness of the implemented solutions. For example, if you have implemented a project management tool, monitor metrics such as project completion time, resource utilization, and client satisfaction. If you have integrated CRM software, track metrics like customer acquisition cost, customer retention rate, and sales conversion rate.

Collect feedback from your team members and customers to gain insights into their experience with the new technology and software solutions. Conduct surveys, hold meetings, and encourage open communication to gather feedback and suggestions for improvement. This feedback will help you identify any issues or challenges and make necessary adjustments to optimize the solutions.

Regularly review and update your technology and software solutions to ensure they remain aligned with your evolving business needs. Technology is constantly evolving, and new solutions may emerge that offer even greater benefits. Stay informed about the latest trends and advancements in your industry and be open to exploring new technologies that can further enhance your business operations.

By implementing technology and software solutions effectively, small business owners can streamline processes, improve efficiency, and achieve their goals more efficiently. Embrace the power of technology and leverage software solutions to propel your business toward success.

5.3 Outsourcing and Delegating Tasks

As a small business owner, it's important to recognize that you can't do everything on your own. In order to maximize your productivity and achieve the results you've dreamed of, you need to learn how to effectively outsource and delegate tasks. This allows you to focus on the core aspects of your business while entrusting other responsibilities to capable individuals or organizations.

5.3.1 Identifying Tasks for Outsourcing

The first step in outsourcing and delegating tasks is to identify which tasks can be effectively handled by someone else. Start by making a list of all the tasks you currently handle in your business. Then, categorize them based on their importance and urgency. This will help you determine which tasks can be outsourced or delegated.

Tasks that are repetitive, time-consuming, or require specialized skills are often good candidates for outsourcing. For example, administrative tasks like data entry, bookkeeping, or customer support can be easily outsourced to virtual assistants or freelancers. On the other hand, tasks that require your expertise or personal touch, such as strategic decision-making or client consultations, should be retained.

5.3.2 Finding the Right Outsourcing Partners

Once you've identified the tasks you want to outsource, the next step is to find the right outsourcing partners. Start by conducting thorough research and due diligence to ensure that the individuals or organizations you choose are reliable, competent, and aligned with your business values.

Consider seeking recommendations from trusted colleagues or industry associations. You can also explore online platforms that connect businesses with freelancers or outsourcing agencies. Look for reviews, testimonials, and portfolios to assess the quality of their work. It's important to establish clear communication channels and set expectations from the beginning to ensure a smooth working relationship.

5.3.3 Delegating Tasks to Your Team

In addition to outsourcing tasks to external partners, it's also crucial to delegate tasks to your internal team members. Delegation not only helps distribute the workload but also empowers your team members to take ownership and develop their skills.

When delegating tasks, it's important to consider the strengths and capabilities of each team member. Assign tasks that align with their expertise and provide them with the necessary resources and support to succeed. Clearly communicate the objectives, expectations, and deadlines for each task. Regularly check in with your team members to provide guidance, feedback, and address any challenges they may encounter.

5.3.4 Benefits of Outsourcing and Delegating

Outsourcing and delegating tasks offer several benefits for small business owners:

1. Increased Efficiency: By outsourcing or delegating tasks, you can focus on high-value activities that directly contribute to the growth and success of your business. This allows you to make the most of your time and expertise.

2. Cost Savings: Outsourcing certain tasks can be more cost-effective than hiring full-time employees. You can save on expenses such as salaries, benefits, and office space. Additionally, outsourcing allows you to access specialized skills without the need for extensive training.

3. Scalability: As your business grows, outsourcing and delegating tasks become even more important. It allows you to scale your operations without overwhelming yourself or your team. You can easily adjust the level of outsourcing based on your business needs.

4. Focus on Core Competencies: By outsourcing non-core tasks, you can focus on the areas where you excel and differentiate yourself from the competition. This helps you maintain a competitive edge in the market.

5. Work-Life Balance: Outsourcing and delegating tasks can help you achieve a better work-life balance. By offloading certain responsibilities, you can free up time for personal activities, relaxation, and spending quality time with loved ones.

5.3.5 Overcoming Challenges

While outsourcing and delegating tasks can be highly beneficial, it's important to be aware of and address potential challenges. Here are some common challenges and strategies to overcome them:

1. Communication: Effective communication is crucial when working with outsourcing partners or delegating tasks to your team. Clearly define expectations, provide detailed instructions, and establish regular check-ins to ensure everyone is on the same page.

2. Trust: Trust is essential when outsourcing tasks to external partners or delegating tasks to your team. Build trust by setting clear expectations, providing support, and recognizing and rewarding achievements.

3. Quality Control: When outsourcing tasks, it's important to establish quality control measures to ensure that the work meets your standards. Regularly review and provide feedback on completed tasks to maintain quality.

4. Time Management: Delegating tasks requires effective time management. Prioritize tasks based on their importance and urgency, and allocate sufficient time for communication, training, and monitoring.

5. Transition Period: When outsourcing or delegating tasks for the first time, there may be a transition period where you and your team members adjust to the new workflow. Be patient and provide support during this period to ensure a smooth transition.

Conclusion

Outsourcing and delegating tasks are essential strategies for small business owners to maximize their productivity and achieve their goals. By identifying tasks for outsourcing, finding the right partners, and effectively delegating tasks to your team, you can focus on the core aspects of your business and drive growth. Embrace the power of outsourcing and delegation to unlock your full potential and take your business to new heights.

5.4 Creating Efficient Workflows

Efficiency is the key to success in any small business. When you have efficient workflows in place, you can maximize productivity, reduce wasted time and resources, and ultimately achieve your goals more quickly. In this section, we will explore the importance of creating efficient workflows and provide practical tips on how to streamline your business processes.

5.4.1 Assessing Your Current Workflows

Before you can create efficient workflows, it's important to assess your current processes. Take a step back and evaluate how tasks are currently being completed in your business. Look for any bottlenecks, redundancies, or areas where tasks are taking longer than necessary. This assessment will help you identify areas for improvement and set the foundation for creating more efficient workflows.

5.4.2 Mapping Out Your Processes

Once you have assessed your current workflows, the next step is to map out your processes. This involves breaking down each task into its individual steps and documenting how they are currently being completed. By visually mapping out your processes, you can identify any unnecessary steps or areas where tasks can be streamlined.

5.4.3 Identifying Areas for Improvement

With your processes mapped out, it's time to identify areas for improvement. Look for tasks that can be automated or delegated to free up time for more important activities. Consider whether certain steps can be eliminated or combined to streamline the workflow. Additionally, seek feedback from your team members who are directly involved in these processes. They may have valuable insights and suggestions for improving efficiency.

5.4.4 Implementing Technology Solutions

Technology can be a powerful tool for creating efficient workflows. Look for software solutions that can automate repetitive tasks, such as customer relationship management (CRM) systems, project management tools, or accounting software. These tools can help streamline your processes, reduce errors, and improve overall efficiency. However, it's important to carefully evaluate and choose the right technology solutions that align with your business needs and goals.

5.4.5 Standardizing Processes

Standardizing processes is another key aspect of creating efficient workflows. By establishing clear and consistent procedures for completing tasks, you can eliminate confusion and reduce errors. Document your processes in a standard operating procedure (SOP) manual that can serve as a reference for your team members. Regularly review and update these procedures to ensure they remain relevant and effective.

5.4.6 Streamlining Communication

Effective communication is essential for efficient workflows. Look for ways to streamline communication within your team and with external stakeholders. Utilize project management tools or collaboration platforms to centralize communication and ensure everyone is on the same page. Encourage open and transparent communication, and establish clear channels for feedback and decision-making.

5.4.7 Training and Empowering Your Team

Efficient workflows rely on a skilled and empowered team. Invest in training and development programs to enhance the skills of your employees. Provide them with the necessary tools and resources to perform their tasks efficiently. Empower your team members to take ownership of their work and encourage them to suggest improvements to the workflow. When your team is equipped and motivated, they can contribute to creating efficient workflows.

5.4.8 Continuous Improvement

Creating efficient workflows is an ongoing process. Regularly review and evaluate your workflows to identify areas for further improvement. Encourage a culture of continuous improvement within your organization, where everyone is encouraged to suggest ideas for streamlining processes. Embrace feedback and be open to making necessary adjustments to optimize efficiency.

5.4.9 Monitoring and Measuring Performance

To ensure the effectiveness of your efficient workflows, it's important to monitor and measure performance. Set key performance indicators (KPIs) that align with your business goals and regularly track progress. Use data and analytics to identify any bottlenecks or areas where further improvements can be made. By monitoring performance, you can make data-driven decisions and continuously optimize your workflows.

5.4.10 Celebrating Success

Finally, don't forget to celebrate the success of your efficient workflows. Recognize and reward your team members for their contributions to streamlining processes. Share success stories and highlight the positive impact that efficient workflows have had on your business. Celebrating success not only boosts morale but also reinforces the importance of creating and maintaining efficient workflows.

By creating efficient workflows, you can maximize productivity, reduce wasted time and resources, and ultimately achieve your goals more quickly. Take the time to assess your current workflows, identify areas for improvement, and implement strategies to streamline your processes. With efficient workflows in place, you can propel your small business toward success.

Chapter Six

6 Multiplying Your Growth

Growth is life. Personal character is more important
than comfort and is the key to long-term success.

6.1 Expanding Your Customer Base

Expanding your customer base is a crucial step in growing your small business. The more customers you have, the more opportunities you have to generate revenue and increase your profits. However, expanding your customer base requires a strategic approach and careful planning. In this section, we will explore effective strategies to help you expand your customer base and attract new customers to your business.

6.1.1 Understanding Your Target Market

Before you can effectively expand your customer base, it is essential to have a clear understanding of your target market. Your target market consists of the specific group of people who are most likely to be interested in your products or services. By understanding your target market, you can tailor your marketing efforts to reach the right audience and attract potential customers.

To understand your target market, you need to conduct market research. This research involves gathering information about your potential customers, such as their demographics, interests, and purchasing behavior. You can gather this information through surveys, interviews, or by analyzing data from your existing customer base.

Once you have a clear understanding of your target market, you can develop targeted marketing campaigns that resonate with your audience. By tailoring your marketing messages to address the specific needs and desires of your target market, you can attract new customers who are more likely to be interested in what you have to offer.

6.1.2 Building an Online Presence

In today's digital age, having a strong online presence is essential for expanding your customer base. The internet provides a vast platform for reaching potential customers and promoting your products or services. Here are some strategies to help you build an effective online presence:

1. Create a professional website: Your website serves as the online face of your business. It should be visually appealing, easy to navigate, and provide relevant information about your products or services. Make sure your website is mo-

bile-friendly, as an increasing number of people access the internet through their smartphones.

2. Optimize for search engines: Search engine optimization (SEO) is the process of improving your website's visibility in search engine results. By optimizing your website for relevant keywords and creating high-quality content, you can increase your chances of appearing in search engine results when potential customers are looking for products or services like yours.

3. Utilize social media: Social media platforms provide an excellent opportunity to connect with your target audience and promote your business. Identify the social media platforms that your target market is most active on and create engaging content that resonates with them. Regularly interact with your followers and respond to their comments or inquiries.

4. Implement email marketing: Email marketing is a powerful tool for nurturing relationships with your existing customers and attracting new ones. Build an email list by offering valuable content or incentives in exchange for email addresses. Send regular newsletters or promotional emails to keep your audience engaged and informed about your products or services.

6.1.3 Networking and Partnerships

Expanding your customer base can also be achieved through networking and forming strategic partnerships. Networking allows you to connect with other professionals in your industry or related industries who may have access to a larger customer base. Here are some networking strategies to consider:

1. Attend industry events and conferences: Participating in industry events and conferences provides an opportunity to meet potential customers and establish valuable connections. Be prepared to introduce yourself and your business, and have your elevator pitch ready to make a lasting impression.

2. Join professional organizations: Joining professional organizations related to your industry can provide access to a network of like-minded individuals who can offer support and potential business opportunities. Attend meetings and events hosted by these organizations to expand your network.

3. Collaborate with complementary businesses: Identify businesses that offer complementary products or services to yours and explore opportunities for collaboration. By partnering with these businesses, you can tap into their customer base and attract new customers who may be interested in what you have to offer.

6.1.4 Providing Exceptional Customer Service

Expanding your customer base is not just about attracting new customers; it is also about retaining existing ones. Providing exceptional customer service is crucial for building customer loyalty and generating positive word-of-mouth referrals. Here are some tips for providing exceptional customer service:

1. Train your staff: Ensure that your employees are well-trained in customer service skills and understand the importance of delivering a positive customer experience. Empower them to resolve customer issues promptly and effectively.

2. Personalize the customer experience: Take the time to understand your customers' needs and preferences. Tailor your interactions and recommendations to meet their specific requirements. Personalization shows that you value your customers and are committed to meeting their individual needs.

3. Respond to feedback: Actively seek feedback from your customers and take their suggestions or concerns seriously. Respond promptly to any feedback, whether positive or negative, and take appropriate action to address any issues raised.

By providing exceptional customer service, you can not only retain your existing customers but also turn them into brand advocates who will recommend your business to others, helping you expand your customer base organically.

Expanding your customer base is an ongoing process that requires continuous effort and adaptation. By understanding your target market, building an online presence, networking, and providing exceptional customer service, you can attract new customers and grow your small business. Remember, expanding your customer base is not just about increasing your revenue; it is about building long-term relationships with your customers and creating a loyal customer base that will support your business for years to come.

6.2 Scaling Your Business Operations

Scaling your business operations is a crucial step in achieving long-term success and growth. As a small business owner, it is essential to have a clear understanding of how to effectively scale your operations to meet the demands of a growing customer base and market. In this section, we will explore strategies and best practices for scaling your business operations using the DREAM Method.

6.2.1 Assessing Your Current Operations

Before you can effectively scale your business operations, it is important to assess your current operations and identify areas that need improvement. Take a close look at your existing processes, systems, and resources to determine their efficiency and effectiveness. This assessment will help you identify any bottlenecks or areas that may hinder your ability to scale.

Evaluate your current workflows, employee roles and responsibilities, and technology infrastructure. Are there any inefficiencies or redundancies that can be eliminated? Are your employees equipped with the necessary skills and tools to handle increased demand? By conducting a thorough assessment, you can identify areas for improvement and develop a plan to scale your operations effectively.

6.2.2 Streamlining Processes and Workflows

Streamlining your processes and workflows is a key component of scaling your business operations. Look for ways to eliminate unnecessary steps, automate repetitive tasks, and improve overall efficiency.

This can involve implementing new technologies, optimizing your supply chain, or reorganizing your team's responsibilities.

Consider adopting project management tools and software that can help streamline communication and collaboration among team members. Automate routine tasks such as invoicing, inventory management, and customer support to free up time for more strategic activities. By streamlining your processes and workflows, you can increase productivity and reduce the risk of errors or delays.

6.2.3 Investing in Technology and Infrastructure

As your business grows, it is crucial to invest in the right technology and infrastructure to support your operations. Evaluate your current technology stack and identify any gaps or areas that need improvement. This may involve upgrading your hardware, implementing new software solutions, or integrating different systems to streamline your operations.

Investing in technology can help you automate processes, improve data management, and enhance customer experience. For example, implementing a customer relationship management (CRM) system can help you track and manage customer interactions more effectively. Adopting cloud-based solutions can provide scalability and flexibility as your business expands. By investing in the right technology and infrastructure, you can position your business for growth and success.

6.2.4 Hiring and Training the Right Talent

Scaling your business operations often requires expanding your team. Hiring and training the right talent is crucial to ensure that your business can handle increased demand and maintain high-quality standards. Assess your current workforce and identify any skill gaps or areas that need reinforcement.

When hiring new employees, look for individuals who align with your company's values and culture. Seek out candidates with the necessary skills and experience to contribute to your business's growth. Provide comprehensive training programs to onboard new employees and ensure they have a clear understanding of their roles and responsibilities.

Additionally, consider cross-training your existing employees to handle multiple tasks and responsibilities. This can help improve flexibility and agility within your team, allowing for smoother operations during periods of growth.

6.2.5 Establishing Scalable Systems and Processes

To effectively scale your business operations, it is essential to establish scalable systems and processes. This involves creating standardized procedures and workflows that can accommodate increased volume and complexity. Document your processes and ensure that they are easily accessible to all team members.

Regularly review and refine your systems and processes to identify areas for improvement. As your business grows, you may need to make adjustments to accommodate changing customer needs and market dynamics. By establishing scalable systems and processes, you can ensure that your business can adapt and grow without sacrificing quality or efficiency.

6.2.6 Monitoring and Measuring Performance

Scaling your business operations requires ongoing monitoring and measurement of key performance indicators (KPIs). Establish clear metrics to track the effectiveness of your scaling efforts and identify areas that need further attention. This can include metrics such as customer satisfaction, employee productivity, and revenue growth.

Regularly review your KPIs and use the data to make informed decisions about your operations. Identify trends and patterns that can help you optimize your processes and allocate resources more effectively. By monitoring and measuring performance, you can ensure that your scaling efforts are on track and make necessary adjustments as needed.

6.2.7 Collaborating with Strategic Partners

Collaborating with strategic partners can be a valuable strategy for scaling your business operations. Look for opportunities to form partnerships with other businesses or professionals who can complement your offerings and help you reach a wider audience. This can involve joint marketing campaigns, cross-promotions, or even strategic alliances.

Strategic partnerships can provide access to new markets, resources, and expertise that can accelerate your growth. Identify potential partners who share similar values and target the same customer base. Establish clear goals and expectations for the partnership to ensure mutual benefits and success.

6.2.8 Managing Cash Flow and Financial Resources

Scaling your business operations requires careful management of cash flow and financial resources. As your business grows, you may need to invest in additional inventory, equipment, or marketing initiatives. It is crucial to have a solid financial plan in place to support your scaling efforts.

Regularly review your financial statements and projections to ensure that you have sufficient funds to support your growth plans. Consider working with a financial advisor or accountant to develop a comprehensive financial strategy. Explore financing options such as loans or lines of credit to bridge any gaps in cash flow.

By effectively managing your cash flow and financial resources, you can ensure that your business has the necessary resources to scale operations and seize growth opportunities.

Conclusion

Scaling your business operations is a critical step in achieving long-term success and growth. By assessing your current operations, streamlining processes, investing in technology, hiring the right talent, establishing scalable systems, monitoring performance, collaborating with strategic partners, and managing cash flow, you can position your business for sustainable growth. Remember, scaling is a continuous process that requires ongoing evaluation and adjustment. Embrace the DREAM Method and take action to scale your business operations and achieve the results you have dreamed of.

6.3 Diversifying Your Product or Service Offerings

Diversifying your product or service offerings is a crucial step in growing your small business and maximizing your success. By expanding your range of products or services, you can attract a wider customer base, increase your revenue streams, and mitigate the risks associated with relying on a single product or service.

6.3.1 Understanding the Benefits of Diversification

Diversification is the process of adding new products or services to your existing offerings. It allows you to tap into new markets, cater to different customer needs, and stay ahead of your competitors. Here are some key benefits of diversifying your product or service offerings:

1. **Increased Revenue**: By offering a variety of products or services, you can generate additional streams of income. This not only boosts your revenue but also provides a buffer against fluctuations in demand for any single product or service.

2. **Expanded Customer Base**: Diversification allows you to reach a broader audience and attract new customers who may have different preferences or needs. By catering to a wider range of customers, you can increase your market share and establish a stronger presence in your industry.

3. **Reduced Risk**: Relying solely on one product or service can be risky, as changes in the market or customer preferences can significantly impact your business. Diversification helps spread the risk by offering multiple products or services, reducing your vulnerability to market fluctuations.

4. **Competitive Advantage**: Offering a diverse range of products or services sets you apart from your competitors. It demonstrates your adaptability and ability to meet the evolving needs of your customers, giving you a competitive

edge in the market.

6.3.2 Identifying Opportunities for Diversification

Before diversifying your product or service offerings, it is essential to conduct thorough market research and identify opportunities that align with your business goals and target audience. Here are some strategies to help you identify potential areas for diversification:

1. **Customer Feedback**: Listen to your customers and understand their needs and preferences. Conduct surveys, gather feedback, and analyze customer data to identify gaps in the market that you can fill with new products or services.

2. **Market Analysis**: Stay updated on industry trends, market demands, and emerging technologies. Analyze your competitors' offerings and identify areas where you can differentiate yourself by providing unique products or services.

3. **Niche Markets**: Explore niche markets that are underserved or have limited competition. By catering to a specific niche, you can position yourself as an expert and capture a dedicated customer base.

4. **Complementary Products or Services**: Consider offering products or services that complement your existing offerings. This allows you to cross-sell and upsell to your existing customer base, increasing customer loyalty and revenue.

6.3.3 Developing a Diversification Strategy

Once you have identified opportunities for diversification, it is crucial to develop a well-defined strategy to ensure successful implementation. Here are some steps to help you develop a diversification strategy:

1. **Set Clear Goals**: Define your objectives for diversification, such as increasing revenue, expanding market share, or entering new markets. Establish measurable goals that align with your overall business strategy.

2. **Evaluate Resources**: Assess your existing resources, including financial, human, and technological capabilities. Determine if you have the necessary resources to support the development and launch of new products or services.

3. **Market Testing**: Before fully committing to a new product or service, conduct market testing to gauge customer interest and demand. This can involve offering a pilot program, conducting focus groups, or running a limited-time promotion to gather feedback and validate your idea.

4. **Develop a Launch Plan**: Create a comprehensive launch plan that outlines the steps, timelines, and resources required to introduce the new product or service. Consider factors such as pricing, marketing strategies, distribution channels, and customer support.

5. **Monitor and Adapt**: Continuously monitor the performance of your new offerings and gather feedback from customers. Analyze sales data, customer satisfaction, and market trends to make necessary adjustments and improvements to your diversification strategy.

6.3.4 Managing the Challenges of Diversification

While diversifying your product or service offerings can bring numerous benefits, it also comes with its own set of challenges. Here are some common challenges and strategies to overcome them:

1. **Resource Allocation**: Diversification requires allocating resources to develop and launch new products or services. Ensure you have a clear understanding of your resource limitations and prioritize investments based on potential returns.

2. **Maintaining Focus**: Diversification can sometimes lead to a loss of focus on your core offerings. It is essential to strike a balance between expanding your offerings and maintaining the quality and consistency of your existing products or services.

3. **Customer Education**: Introducing new products or services may require educating your customers about their benefits and value. Develop effective marketing and communication strategies to educate and engage your target audience.

4. **Managing Complexity**: Diversification can increase the complexity of your business operations. Implement efficient systems and processes to manage the additional workload and ensure smooth integration of new offerings into your existing business structure.

By diversifying your product or service offerings, you can unlock new growth opportunities and position your small business for long-term success. Remember to conduct thorough research, develop a clear strategy, and monitor the performance of your new offerings to maximize the benefits of diversification.

6.4 Investing in Marketing and Advertising

Marketing and advertising play a crucial role in the success of any small business. It is through effective marketing and advertising strategies that you can reach your target audience, build brand awareness, and ultimately drive sales. In this section, we will explore the importance of investing in marketing and advertising and provide you with practical tips on how to make the most out of your marketing budget.

6.4.1 Understanding the Importance of Marketing

Marketing is the process of promoting and selling products or services to customers. It encompasses various activities such as market research, product development, pricing, distribution, and promotion. Effective marketing allows you to communicate the value of your products or services to your target audience and differentiate yourself from competitors.

Investing in marketing is essential for small businesses because it helps you:

1. **Build brand awareness**: Marketing efforts such as advertising, social media, and content marketing help you create brand recognition and establish your business as a trusted and reputable source.

2. **Reach your target audience**: By understanding your target market and their needs, you can tailor your marketing messages and channels to effectively reach and engage with your ideal customers.

3. **Generate leads and drive sales**: Marketing activities such

as lead generation campaigns, email marketing, and sales promotions can help you attract potential customers and convert them into paying customers.

4. **Build customer loyalty**: Through ongoing marketing efforts, you can nurture relationships with your existing customers, encourage repeat purchases, and foster brand loyalty.

6.4.2 Defining Your Marketing Goals

Before investing in marketing and advertising, it is crucial to define your goals. Your marketing goals should align with your overall business objectives and be specific, measurable, achievable, relevant, and time-bound (SMART). Here are some common marketing goals for small businesses:

1. **Increase brand awareness**: If your business is relatively new or you want to expand your reach, your goal may be to increase brand awareness by a certain percentage within a specific timeframe.

2. **Generate leads**: If your focus is on acquiring new customers, your goal may be to generate a certain number of leads per month or quarter.

3. **Drive website traffic**: If your business relies heavily on online sales or lead generation, your goal may be to increase website traffic by a certain percentage.

4. **Boost sales**: If your primary objective is to increase revenue, your goal may be to achieve a specific sales target within a given period.

By setting clear and measurable goals, you can track your progress and make data-driven decisions to optimize your marketing efforts.

6.4.3 Developing Your Marketing Strategy

Once you have defined your marketing goals, it's time to develop a comprehensive marketing strategy. Your marketing strategy outlines the specific tactics and channels you will use to achieve your goals. Here are some key steps to consider when developing your marketing strategy:

1. **Identify your target audience**: Understand who your ideal customers are, their demographics, interests, and pain points. This will help you tailor your marketing messages and choose the most effective channels to reach them.

2. **Research your competitors**: Analyze your competitors' marketing strategies to identify gaps and opportunities. This will help you differentiate your business and develop a unique value proposition.

3. **Choose the right marketing channels**: Consider the most effective marketing channels for your target audience. This may include a combination of online channels such as social media, search engine optimization (SEO), content marketing, email marketing, and offline channels such as print advertising, events, and direct mail.

4. **Create compelling content**: Develop high-quality content that resonates with your target audience. This can include blog posts, videos, infographics, case studies, and customer testimonials. Compelling content helps build trust, establish

thought leadership, and drive engagement.

5. **Set a budget**: Determine how much you are willing to invest in marketing and allocate your budget across different channels and tactics. It's important to track your marketing expenses and measure the return on investment (ROI) for each marketing activity.

6. **Track and analyze results**: Regularly monitor and analyze the performance of your marketing campaigns. Use analytics tools to measure key metrics such as website traffic, conversion rates, email open rates, and social media engagement. This data will help you identify what's working and what needs improvement.

6.4.4 Leveraging Digital Marketing

In today's digital age, digital marketing has become an essential component of any marketing strategy. Digital marketing encompasses various online tactics and channels that allow you to reach a wider audience and engage with them on a more personal level. Here are some key digital marketing tactics to consider:

1. **Search engine optimization (SEO)**: Optimize your website and content to rank higher in search engine results. This will increase your visibility and organic traffic.

2. **Social media marketing**: Leverage social media platforms such as Facebook, Instagram, Twitter, and LinkedIn to connect with your target audience, share valuable content, and promote your products or services.

3. **Email marketing**: Build an email list and send targeted email campaigns to nurture leads, promote new products or services, and drive sales.

4. **Pay-per-click (PPC) advertising**: Run targeted ads on search engines or social media platforms to drive traffic to your website or landing pages. PPC advertising allows you to reach a specific audience and only pay when someone clicks on your ad.

5. **Content marketing**: Create and distribute valuable and relevant content to attract and engage your target audience. This can include blog posts, videos, podcasts, and infographics.

6. **Influencer marketing**: Collaborate with influencers or industry experts who have a significant following to promote your products or services. Influencer marketing can help you reach a wider audience and build credibility.

Remember, digital marketing is constantly evolving, so it's important to stay updated with the latest trends and tactics to ensure your marketing efforts remain effective.

Investing in marketing and advertising is a critical step in growing your small business. By understanding the importance of marketing, defining your goals, developing a comprehensive marketing strategy, and leveraging digital marketing tactics, you can maximize your marketing budget and achieve the results you have dreamed of.

7 Creating Worry-Free Wealth

Money shouldn't be the goal. It's the freedom that comes from having peace of mind that we're after.

7.1 Financial Planning and Budgeting

F inancial planning and budgeting are essential components of small business success. As a small business owner, it is crucial to have a clear understanding of your financial situation and to develop a strategic plan to manage your resources effectively. In this section, we will explore the importance of financial planning and budgeting and provide practical tips to help you create a solid financial foundation for your business.

7.1.1 Assessing Your Current Financial Situation

Before you can create a financial plan and budget for your small business, it is important to assess your current financial situation. This involves gathering and analyzing information about your income, expenses, assets, and liabilities. By understanding your financial position, you can make informed decisions and set realistic financial goals for your business.

Start by reviewing your financial statements, such as your income statement, balance sheet, and cash flow statement. These statements will provide you with a snapshot of your business's financial health and help you identify areas that need improvement. Additionally, consider your current debt obligations, including loans and credit card balances, as these will impact your cash flow and ability to invest in your business.

7.1.2 Setting Financial Goals

Once you have assessed your current financial situation, it is time to set financial goals for your small business. Financial goals provide a roadmap for your business's financial success and help you stay focused and motivated. When setting financial goals, it is important to make them specific, measurable, achievable, relevant, and time-bound (SMART). For example, instead of setting a vague goal like "increase revenue," set a specific goal like "increase monthly revenue by 10% within the next six months."

Consider both short-term and long-term financial goals. Short-term goals may include reducing expenses, increasing cash flow, or paying off debt, while long-term goals may involve saving for expansion, investing in new equipment, or building a retirement fund. By setting a combination of short-term and long-term goals, you can create a balanced financial plan that addresses both immediate needs and future growth.

7.1.3 Creating a Budget

A budget is a financial plan that outlines your projected income and expenses over a specific period. It serves as a roadmap for managing your business's finances and helps you allocate resources effectively. To create a budget, start by estimating your expected income from sales, investments, and other sources. Then, identify and categorize your expenses, including fixed costs (rent, utilities, salaries) and variable costs (inventory, marketing, supplies).

Once you have identified your income and expenses, compare them to determine if you have a surplus or a deficit. If you have a surplus, consider allocating the excess funds toward savings, debt repayment, or investments. If you have a deficit, look for areas where you can reduce expenses or increase revenue to achieve a balanced budget.

Regularly review and update your budget to reflect changes in your business's financial situation. This will help you stay on track and make necessary adjustments to achieve your financial goals. Additionally, consider using budgeting software or apps to streamline the budgeting process and track your expenses more efficiently.

7.1.4 Managing Cash Flow

Cash flow management is a critical aspect of financial planning for small businesses. It involves monitoring and controlling the flow of cash in and out of your business to ensure you have enough funds to cover expenses and invest in growth opportunities. Poor cash flow management can lead to financial difficulties and hinder your business's ability to thrive.

To effectively manage cash flow, start by forecasting your cash inflows and outflows on a monthly or quarterly basis. This will help you anticipate periods of high and low cash flow and make necessary adjustments to ensure you have enough liquidity to meet your financial obligations. Consider implementing strategies to accelerate cash inflows, such as offering discounts for early payments or implementing a more efficient invoicing system.

On the expense side, prioritize your payments based on their importance and urgency. This will help you allocate your available funds to critical expenses, such as payroll and rent, while delaying non-essential expenses if necessary. Additionally, consider negotiating favorable payment terms with your suppliers to improve your cash flow position.

Regularly monitor your cash flow and compare it to your budget to identify any discrepancies or areas for improvement. By staying proactive and vigilant in managing your cash flow, you can avoid cash shortages and maintain a healthy financial position for your small business.

7.1.5 Seeking Professional Advice

Financial planning and budgeting can be complex, especially for small business owners who may not have a background in finance. If you feel overwhelmed or unsure about managing your business's finances, consider seeking professional advice from an accountant or financial advisor. These professionals can provide valuable insights and guidance tailored to your specific business needs.

When choosing a financial professional, look for someone with experience working with small businesses in your industry. They should have a deep understanding of tax regulations, financial analysis, and business planning. Additionally, consider their communication style and availability to ensure a good working relationship.

Remember, financial planning and budgeting are ongoing processes. As your business evolves and grows, your financial goals and strategies may need to be adjusted. Stay proactive, regularly review your financial plan, and make necessary changes to ensure your business's long-term financial success. By mastering financial planning and budgeting, you will be well-equipped to achieve your business goals and create worry-free wealth.

7.2 Investing and Wealth Management

As a small business owner, it's important to not only focus on the day-to-day operations of your business but also to plan for your financial future. Investing and wealth management play a crucial role in ensuring long-term financial stability and success. In this section, we will explore the key principles and strategies for effective investing and wealth management.

7.2.1 Understanding the Importance of Investing

Investing is the process of allocating your resources, such as money, time, and effort, with the expectation of generating a return or profit in the future. It is a crucial component of building wealth and achieving financial independence. By investing wisely, you can grow your assets and create a secure financial foundation for yourself and your business.

7.2.2 Setting Financial Goals

Before you start investing, it's important to set clear financial goals. These goals will serve as a roadmap for your investment strategy and help you stay focused on your long-term objectives. Whether your goals include saving for retirement, funding your children's education, or expanding your business, having a clear vision of what you want to achieve will guide your investment decisions.

7.2.3 Assessing Your Risk Tolerance

Investing involves taking on a certain level of risk. Understanding your risk tolerance is essential in determining the types of investments that are suitable for you. Some individuals are comfortable with higher levels of risk and are willing to invest in more volatile assets, while others prefer a more conservative approach. Assessing your risk tolerance will help you create an investment portfolio that aligns with your comfort level and financial goals.

7.2.4 Diversification

Diversification is a fundamental principle of investing. It involves spreading your investments across different asset classes, industries, and geographic regions to reduce the risk of loss. By diversifying your portfolio, you can potentially minimize the impact of any single investment's performance on your overall wealth. This strategy allows you to capture the upside potential of different markets while mitigating the downside risk.

7.2.5 Investment Vehicles

There are various investment vehicles available to small business owners, each with its own characteristics and risk profiles. Some common investment options include stocks, bonds, mutual funds, exchange-traded funds (ETFs), real estate, and commodities. It's important to understand the features and risks associated with each investment vehicle before making any investment decisions. Consulting with a financial advisor can help you navigate the complexities of different investment options and choose the ones that align with your goals and risk tolerance.

7.2.6 Long-Term Investing

Successful investing requires a long-term perspective. While short-term market fluctuations can be unsettling, it's important to stay focused on your long-term goals and not be swayed by temporary market volatility. By adopting a long-term investment strategy, you can benefit from the power of compounding and ride out market cycles. Regularly reviewing and rebalancing your portfolio can help ensure that it remains aligned with your long-term objectives.

7.2.7 Monitoring and Adjusting Your Investments

Investing is not a set-it-and-forget-it activity. It requires ongoing monitoring and periodic adjustments to ensure that your investments continue to align with your goals and risk tolerance. Regularly reviewing your portfolio's performance, staying informed about market trends, and making necessary adjustments can help you optimize your investment returns and mitigate potential risks.

7.2.8 Seeking Professional Advice

Investing can be complex, especially for small business owners who are already juggling multiple responsibilities. Seeking professional advice from a qualified financial advisor can provide valuable insights and guidance. A financial advisor can help you develop a personalized investment strategy, assess your risk tolerance, and navigate the ever-changing investment landscape. They can also provide ongoing support and help you stay on track toward achieving your financial goals.

7.2.9 Managing Wealth and Protecting Assets

Wealth management goes beyond investing. It involves comprehensive financial planning, including tax planning, estate planning, and risk management. As a small business owner, it's important to protect your assets and ensure that your wealth is preserved for future generations. Working with a team of professionals, including financial advisors, accountants, and attorneys, can help you develop a holistic wealth management strategy that addresses all aspects of your financial well-being.

7.2.10 Continual Learning and Adaptation

The world of investing is constantly evolving, and it's important to stay informed and adapt to changing market conditions. Continual learning about investment strategies, market trends, and new opportunities can help you make informed decisions and maximize your investment returns. Additionally, regularly reviewing and updating your investment plan based on your changing financial circumstances and goals is essential for long-term success.

In conclusion, investing and wealth management are essential components of small business success. By setting clear financial goals, understanding your risk tolerance, diversifying your investments, and seeking professional advice, you can create a solid foundation for long-term financial stability. Continual learning, monitoring, and adjusting your investments will help you adapt to changing market conditions and maximize your investment returns. Remember, investing is a journey, and with the right strategies and mindset, you can achieve your financial dreams.

7.3 Building Multiple Streams of Income

As a small business owner, one of the keys to long-term success and financial stability is building multiple streams of income. Relying solely on one source of revenue can be risky, as it leaves you vulnerable to market fluctuations, changes in consumer behavior, and unexpected challenges. By diversifying your income streams, you can create a more stable and resilient business that can weather any storm.

7.3.1 Why Multiple Streams of Income Matter

Having multiple streams of income provides several benefits for small business owners. Firstly, it reduces the risk of relying on a single source of revenue. If one income stream experiences a downturn, you have other sources to fall back on, ensuring that your business can continue to generate income.

Secondly, multiple streams of income can increase your overall earning potential. By diversifying your revenue sources, you have the opportunity to tap into different markets, target different customer segments, and offer a variety of products or services. This can lead to increased sales and profitability.

Additionally, building multiple streams of income allows you to explore new opportunities and expand your business. It opens doors to partnerships, collaborations, and joint ventures that can further enhance your growth potential. It also provides a platform for innovation and experimentation, as you can test new ideas and ventures without jeopardizing your entire business.

7.3.2 Types of Multiple Income Streams

There are various ways to build multiple streams of income for your small business. Here are some common strategies to consider:

7.3.2.1 Diversify Product or Service Offerings

One way to create additional income streams is by diversifying your product or service offerings. This involves expanding your range of offerings to cater to different customer needs and preferences. For example, if you own a bakery, you could consider adding specialty cakes, catering services, or baking classes to your existing product line. By diversifying your offerings, you can attract new customers and generate additional revenue.

7.3.2.2 Create Passive Income Streams

Passive income streams are a great way to generate income with minimal ongoing effort. This can include income from rental properties, royalties from intellectual property, affiliate marketing, or online courses. Passive income streams allow you to earn money even when you're not actively working, providing a steady source of income that can supplement your primary business.

7.3.2.3 Explore Partnerships and Joint Ventures

Collaborating with other businesses through partnerships and joint ventures can be a powerful way to create new income streams. By combining resources, expertise, and customer bases, you can tap into new markets and reach a wider audience. For example, if you own a fitness studio, you could partner with a nutritionist to offer joint packages or collaborate with a local spa to create wellness retreats. These partnerships can not only generate additional income but also strengthen your brand and reputation.

7.3.2.4 Leverage Digital Platforms

In today's digital age, there are numerous opportunities to generate income online. Whether it's through e-commerce, affiliate marketing, or creating and selling digital products, leveraging digital platforms can open up new income streams for your business. Consider setting up an online store, creating a blog or YouTube channel, or offering online consulting services to reach a global audience and increase your earning potential.

7.3.3 Implementing Multiple Streams of Income

Building multiple streams of income requires careful planning and execution. Here are some steps to help you implement this strategy effectively:

7.3.3.1 Evaluate Your Current Business

Start by evaluating your current business and identifying areas where you can expand or diversify. Consider your existing customer base, resources, and expertise. Look for opportunities to leverage your strengths and fill gaps in the market.

7.3.3.2 Research and Identify Income Opportunities

Research different income opportunities that align with your business and target market. Look for trends, emerging markets, and customer demands that you can tap into. Consider the feasibility, profitability, and scalability of each opportunity before making a decision.

7.3.3.3 Develop a Strategic Plan

Once you have identified potential income streams, develop a strategic plan to implement them. Set clear goals, define target markets, and outline the steps needed to launch and manage each income stream. Consider the resources, time, and investment required for each opportunity.

7.3.3.4 Test and Refine

Before fully committing to a new income stream, test it on a smaller scale to gauge its viability and profitability. Collect feedback from customers, track sales and revenue, and make necessary adjustments to optimize performance. Continuously monitor and refine your strategies to ensure long-term success.

7.3.3.5 Monitor and Manage

Once you have multiple income streams in place, it's important to regularly monitor and manage them. Keep track of sales, expenses, and profitability for each stream. Identify any challenges or opportunities for improvement and take proactive measures to optimize performance.

Conclusion

Building multiple streams of income is a strategic approach that can provide stability, growth, and financial security for your small business. By diversifying your revenue sources, exploring new opportunities, and leveraging digital platforms, you can create a resilient business that can adapt to changing market conditions and maximize your earning potential. Implementing multiple streams of income requires careful planning, research, and ongoing management, but the rewards can be significant. Start exploring new income opportunities today and take your business to new heights of success.

7.4 Protecting Your Assets and Managing Risks

As a small business owner, protecting your assets and managing risks is crucial for the long-term success and sustainability of your business. In this section, we will explore strategies and best practices to safeguard your assets and mitigate potential risks.

7.4.1 Assessing and Identifying Risks

The first step in protecting your assets and managing risks is to assess and identify potential risks that your business may face. This involves conducting a thorough analysis of your business operations, processes, and external factors that could impact your business.

Start by identifying the different types of risks that your business may encounter. These can include financial risks, operational risks, legal risks, market risks, and reputational risks, among others. Once you have identified the risks, evaluate the likelihood of each risk occurring and the potential impact it could have on your business.

7.4.2 Developing a Risk Management Plan

Once you have identified the risks, it is essential to develop a comprehensive risk management plan. This plan should outline the strategies and actions you will take to mitigate and manage the identified risks effectively.

Start by prioritizing the risks based on their potential impact on your business. Focus on addressing the risks that pose the highest threat first. Develop specific strategies and measures to minimize the likelihood of these risks occurring and to reduce their potential impact.

Your risk management plan should also include contingency plans for dealing with unexpected events or emergencies. These plans should outline the steps you will take to minimize the impact of such events on your business operations and finances.

7.4.3 Insurance Coverage

Insurance is a critical component of protecting your assets and managing risks. It provides financial protection in the event of unforeseen circumstances or accidents that could result in significant financial losses for your business.

Evaluate the different types of insurance coverage available and determine which ones are most relevant to your business. Common types of insurance for small businesses include general liability insurance, property insurance, professional liability insurance, and workers' compensation insurance, among others.

Consult with an insurance professional to ensure that you have the appropriate coverage for your business needs. Regularly review your insurance policies to ensure they are up to date and provide adequate coverage as your business grows and evolves.

7.4.4 Legal Compliance

Complying with applicable laws and regulations is essential for protecting your assets and managing risks. Failure to comply with legal requirements can result in fines, penalties, and legal disputes that can have a significant impact on your business.

Stay informed about the laws and regulations that apply to your industry and business operations. Regularly review and update your business practices to ensure compliance. Seek legal advice when necessary to ensure that you are meeting all legal obligations.

Additionally, consider implementing internal controls and procedures to prevent fraud, theft, and other illegal activities within your business. This can include implementing strong financial controls, conducting regular audits, and providing training to employees on ethical business practices.

7.4.5 Cybersecurity

In today's digital age, protecting your business from cyber threats is essential. Cybersecurity breaches can result in significant financial losses, reputational damage, and legal liabilities.

Implement robust cybersecurity measures to safeguard your business's sensitive information and data. This can include using secure passwords, regularly updating software and systems, encrypting data, and implementing firewalls and antivirus software.

Educate yourself and your employees about common cybersecurity threats and best practices for preventing cyber attacks. Regularly review and update your cybersecurity protocols to stay ahead of evolving threats.

7.4.6 Business Continuity Planning

Business continuity planning involves developing strategies and procedures to ensure that your business can continue operating in the event of a disruption or crisis. This is crucial for protecting your assets and minimizing the impact of unexpected events on your business.

Identify the potential risks and disruptions that could affect your business, such as natural disasters, power outages, or supply chain disruptions. Develop contingency plans and procedures to ensure that your business can continue operating or recover quickly in the face of these challenges.

Regularly review and update your business continuity plans to reflect changes in your business operations and external factors. Test your plans periodically to ensure their effectiveness and make any necessary adjustments.

7.4.7 Regular Monitoring and Review

Protecting your assets and managing risks is an ongoing process. Regular monitoring and review of your risk management strategies and practices are essential to ensure their effectiveness and make any necessary adjustments.

Schedule regular reviews of your risk management plan to assess its effectiveness and identify any new risks that may have emerged. Stay informed about industry trends, regulatory changes, and other external factors that could impact your business's risk profile.

Continuously educate yourself and your team about risk management best practices and emerging risks. Encourage a culture of risk awareness and proactive risk management within your organization.

By implementing these strategies and best practices, you can protect your assets and effectively manage risks, ensuring the long-term success and sustainability of your small business. Remember, risk management is an ongoing process that requires regular attention and adaptation to changing circumstances.

Chapter Eight

8 Conclusion

Learning from where you've been is often the first step
to moving forward.

If you'd like help implementing these strategies in your life, visit me
at **RHCoaches.com** to get started

8.1 Reviewing Your Progress and Celebrating Success

Congratulations! You have come a long way on your journey toward small business success. As a small business owner, it is essential to regularly review your progress and celebrate your achievements. This not only allows you to acknowledge your hard work but also provides an opportunity to reflect on your journey and make any necessary adjustments to your goals and strategies.

Reflecting on Your Goals

Take a moment to revisit the goals you set for yourself and your business. Are you on track to achieving them? Have you encountered any unexpected challenges or opportunities along the way? Reflecting on your goals allows you to assess your progress and make any necessary adjustments.

One effective way to review your progress is by breaking down your goals into smaller milestones. This allows you to track your progress more easily and provides a sense of accomplishment as you achieve each milestone. Celebrate these milestones as they serve as reminders of your progress and motivate you to keep moving forward.

Assessing Your Strategies

In addition to reviewing your goals, it is crucial to assess the effectiveness of the strategies you have implemented. Are they yielding the desired results? Are there any areas where you can improve or refine your approach?

Consider gathering feedback from your team, customers, or mentors to gain different perspectives on your strategies. This feedback can provide valuable insights and help you identify areas for improvement. Remember, continuous improvement is key to long-term success.

Recognizing Achievements

Celebrating your successes, no matter how small, is an essential part of the journey toward small business success. Recognizing and acknowledging your achievements not only boosts morale but also reinforces positive behaviors and motivates you to continue striving for excellence.

Create a culture of celebration within your business. This can be as simple as acknowledging individual and team accomplishments during regular meetings or hosting special events to commemorate significant milestones. By celebrating your achievements, you create a positive and supportive environment that encourages growth and fosters a sense of pride among your team.

Learning from Setbacks

While celebrating success is important, it is equally crucial to learn from setbacks and failures. Small business ownership is not without its challenges, and setbacks are inevitable. However, it is how you respond to these setbacks that will ultimately determine your success.

When faced with a setback, take the time to analyze what went wrong and identify any lessons that can be learned. Use setbacks as opportunities for growth and improvement. By embracing a growth mindset and viewing setbacks as learning experiences, you can turn adversity into an opportunity for future success.

Setting New Goals

As you review your progress and celebrate your achievements, it is also important to set new goals for yourself and your business. Setting new goals keeps you motivated and focused on continuous improvement.

When setting new goals, consider the lessons you have learned from your past experiences. Use this knowledge to set realistic and achievable goals that align with your long-term vision. Remember to make your goals specific, measurable, attainable, relevant, and time-bound (SMART) to increase your chances of success.

Celebrating Milestones

In addition to celebrating the achievement of your goals, it is important to celebrate the milestones along the way. Milestones represent significant moments of progress and deserve recognition.

Create a system for tracking and celebrating milestones within your business. This can be as simple as a visual representation of your progress or a dedicated space where you display your achievements. Celebrating milestones not only boosts morale but also serves as a reminder of how far you have come and motivates you to keep pushing forward.

Cultivating a Growth Mindset

Maintaining motivation and a growth mindset is essential for long-term success. As a small business owner, you will face numerous challenges and obstacles along the way. It is important to approach these challenges with a positive and resilient mindset.

Cultivate a growth mindset by embracing the belief that you can learn and grow from every experience. Surround yourself with positive and supportive individuals who inspire and motivate you. Continuously seek opportunities for personal and professional development to enhance your skills and knowledge.

Celebrating Success with Others

As you celebrate your own success, remember to pay it forward and inspire others. Share your journey, lessons learned, and achievements with fellow small business owners and aspiring entrepreneurs. By sharing your experiences, you can provide guidance and inspiration to others who may be on a similar path.

Consider hosting workshops, speaking engagements, or mentoring programs to share your knowledge and expertise. Celebrating success with others not only benefits the wider business community but also reinforces your achievements and solidifies your position as a leader in your industry.

In conclusion, reviewing your progress and celebrating success is an integral part of the small business journey. Take the time to reflect on your goals, assess your strategies, and recognize your achievements. Learn from setbacks, set new goals, and celebrate milestones along the way. Cultivate a growth mindset and share your success with others. By doing so, you will not only maximize your potential but also inspire and uplift those around you.

8.2 Maintaining Motivation and Continuous Improvement

Maintaining motivation and continuously improving yourself and your business are crucial aspects of achieving long-term success. In this section, we will explore strategies and techniques to help you stay motivated and continuously grow as a small business owner.

8.2.1 Cultivating a Growth Mindset

One of the key factors in maintaining motivation and continuous improvement is cultivating a growth mindset. A growth mindset is the belief that your abilities and intelligence can be developed through dedication and hard work. It is the understanding that failure and setbacks are opportunities for learning and growth.

To cultivate a growth mindset, it is important to embrace challenges and view them as opportunities for growth. Instead of being discouraged by obstacles, see them as stepping stones toward success. Embrace a positive attitude toward learning and seek out new knowledge and skills that can help you improve your business.

8.2.2 Setting Stretch Goals

Setting stretch goals is another effective way to maintain motivation and drive continuous improvement. Stretch goals are ambitious targets that go beyond what you think is currently possible. By setting stretch goals, you push yourself and your business to reach new heights and achieve more than you thought was possible.

When setting stretch goals, it is important to ensure they are still attainable with effort and dedication. Break down these goals into smaller milestones and create a plan to achieve them. Celebrate each milestone along the way to keep yourself motivated and inspired.

8.2.3 Tracking Progress and Celebrating Success

Tracking your progress and celebrating your successes is essential for maintaining motivation and continuous improvement. Regularly review your goals and assess how far you have come. This will not only help you stay motivated but also provide valuable insights into areas where you can improve.

Create a system for tracking your progress, whether it's through a spreadsheet, a project management tool, or a journal. Set regular checkpoints to evaluate your progress and make adjustments to your strategies if needed. Celebrate your achievements, no matter how small, as they are stepping stones toward your ultimate success.

8.2.4 Seeking Feedback and Learning from Others

Continuous improvement requires a willingness to seek feedback and learn from others. Surround yourself with a supportive network of mentors, peers, and industry experts who can provide valuable insights and guidance. Actively seek feedback from your customers, employees, and partners to gain different perspectives and identify areas for improvement.

Be open to constructive criticism and view it as an opportunity to grow. Embrace a culture of learning within your business and encourage your team members to share their ideas and suggestions. By learning from others and incorporating their feedback, you can continuously improve your business and stay ahead of the competition.

8.2.5 Investing in Personal and Professional Development

Investing in your personal and professional development is crucial for maintaining motivation and continuous improvement. Attend workshops, seminars, and conferences related to your industry to stay updated on the latest trends and best practices. Consider joining professional associations or networking groups to connect with like-minded individuals and expand your knowledge.

Additionally, allocate time for self-reflection and self-improvement. Set aside time each day or week to read books, listen to podcasts, or engage in activities that inspire and motivate you. Develop new skills that are relevant to your business and explore new areas of interest that can contribute to your personal and professional growth.

8.2.6 Embracing Failure as a Learning Opportunity

Failure is an inevitable part of the journey toward success. Instead of being discouraged by failure, embrace it as a learning opportunity. Analyze what went wrong, identify the lessons learned, and use that knowledge to improve your strategies and decision-making.

Encourage a culture of experimentation and innovation within your business. Create an environment where failure is seen as a stepping stone toward success, rather than a reason to give up. By embracing failure and learning from it, you can continuously improve and adapt your business to changing circumstances.

8.2.7 Celebrating Milestones and Recognizing Achievements

Along the journey toward your goals, it is important to celebrate milestones and recognize achievements. Take the time to acknowledge and appreciate the progress you have made. Celebrate not only your own achievements but also those of your team members and employees.

Recognition can come in various forms, such as verbal praise, rewards, or team celebrations. By celebrating milestones and recognizing achievements, you create a positive and motivating work environment. This, in turn, fosters a sense of accomplishment and encourages everyone to strive for continuous improvement.

8.2.8 Embracing Continuous Learning and Adaptation

In today's rapidly changing business landscape, it is crucial to embrace continuous learning and adaptation. Stay updated on industry trends, technological advancements, and changes in consumer behavior. Be open to new ideas and be willing to adapt your strategies and processes accordingly.

Encourage a culture of innovation within your business. Foster an environment where new ideas are welcomed and experimentation is encouraged. Regularly evaluate your business processes and seek opportunities for improvement. By embracing continuous learning and adaptation, you can stay ahead of the competition and drive continuous improvement.

8.2.9 Taking Care of Your Well-being

Maintaining motivation and continuous improvement requires taking care of your well-being. Prioritize self-care and ensure you have a healthy work-life balance. Take breaks, exercise regularly, and engage in activities that help you relax and recharge.

Additionally, surround yourself with a supportive network of family and friends who can provide emotional support. Seek professional help if you are feeling overwhelmed or experiencing burnout. Remember, your well-being is essential for your success as a small business owner.

In conclusion, maintaining motivation and continuously improving yourself and your business are vital for long-term success. Cultivate a growth mindset, set stretch goals, track your progress, seek feedback, invest in personal and professional development, embrace failure as a learning opportunity, celebrate milestones, and adapt to change. By incorporating these strategies into your business practices, you can stay motivated, continuously improve, and achieve the success you have dreamed of.

8.3 Taking Action and Implementing the DREAM Method

Now that you have learned about the DREAM Method and how it can help you achieve your small business goals, it's time to take action and implement this powerful framework. In this section, we will discuss the steps you need to take to effectively apply the DREAM Method to your business and start seeing real results.

8.3.1 Start with Discovering Your Goals

The first step in implementing the DREAM Method is to discover your goals. Take the time to reflect on what you truly want to achieve with your small business. Identify your passions and values, and align your goals with them. Setting both long-term and short-term goals will give you a clear direction and a sense of purpose. Prioritize your goals based on their importance and urgency, and break them down into manageable tasks. By clearly defining your goals, you will have a roadmap to follow and a clear vision of what you want to achieve.

8.3.2 Remove Your Obstacles

Once you have identified your goals, it's time to remove the obstacles that may be standing in your way. Identify and overcome any limiting beliefs that may be holding you back. Challenge yourself to step out of your comfort zone and take calculated risks. Develop effective time management skills to overcome procrastination and make the most of your time. Manage stress and overcome fear by practicing self-care and adopting stress management techniques. Building a supportive network of like-minded individuals who can provide guidance and encouragement will also help you overcome obstacles and stay motivated.

8.3.3 Enhance Your Strategies

To achieve your goals, it's important to enhance your strategies. Develop effective planning and organization skills to stay on track and make the most of your resources. Improve your decision-making and problem-solving abilities to overcome challenges and make informed choices. Utilize effective communication and negotiation skills to build strong relationships with your team, customers, and stakeholders. Embrace change and innovation to stay ahead of the competition and adapt to evolving market trends. By continuously enhancing your strategies, you will be better equipped to navigate the ever-changing business landscape.

8.3.4 Automate Your Systems

Automation is a key aspect of the DREAM Method. Streamline your business processes by identifying areas that can be automated. Implement technology and software solutions that can help you save time and increase efficiency. Consider outsourcing and delegating tasks that can be handled by others, allowing you to focus on high-value activities. Create efficient workflows that minimize manual work and maximize productivity. By automating your systems, you can free up valuable time and resources to focus on strategic initiatives and business growth.

8.3.5 Multiply Your Growth and Create Worry-Free Wealth

The final step in implementing the DREAM Method is to multiply your growth and create worry-free wealth. Expand your customer base by implementing effective marketing and advertising strategies. Scale your business operations to meet the growing demands of your customers. Diversify your product or service offerings to cater to a wider audience and reduce dependency on a single revenue stream. Invest in financial planning and budgeting to ensure long-term financial stability. Explore investment opportunities and wealth management strategies to grow your wealth. Protect your assets and manage risks by implementing appropriate risk management strategies. By multiplying your growth and creating worry-free wealth, you can secure the future of your small business.

Conclusion

Implementing the DREAM Method requires dedication, perseverance, and a commitment to taking action. By following the steps outlined in this section, you will be well on your way to achieving success and crossing the rivers that await you. Remember to review your progress regularly, celebrate your successes, and maintain motivation for continuous improvement. As you implement the DREAM Method and achieve your goals, don't forget to inspire others and pay it forward. Share your knowledge and experiences with fellow small business owners, and help them realize their dreams as well. With the DREAM Method, you have the tools and strategies to turn your dreams into reality. So, take action today and start building the bridge of your dreams.

8.4 Inspiring Others and Paying It Forward

As a small business owner, achieving your goals and dreams is not just about personal success. It's also about inspiring others and making a positive impact in the world. When you have experienced the power of goal mastery and the success it brings, it's important to share your knowledge and help others along their own journey. By paying it forward, you not only uplift others but also create a ripple effect of success and fulfillment.

8.4.1 The Power of Inspiration

Inspiration is a powerful force that can ignite passion and drive in others. When you share your story and the strategies that have helped you achieve your goals, you have the ability to inspire and motivate others to take action. By showing them what is possible, you can help them overcome their own obstacles and reach new heights of success.

One of the most effective ways to inspire others is through storytelling. Share your own experiences, challenges, and triumphs. Be authentic and vulnerable, as this will resonate with others on a deeper level. When people can relate to your journey, they are more likely to believe in their own potential and take action toward their goals.

8.4.2 Becoming a Mentor

Mentoring is a powerful way to inspire and guide others on their path to success. By sharing your knowledge, skills, and expertise, you can help others avoid common pitfalls and accelerate their progress. As a mentor, you have the opportunity to provide guidance, support, and accountability to those who are just starting out or facing challenges in their own businesses.

When mentoring others, it's important to listen actively and empathetically. Understand their unique goals, challenges, and aspirations. Offer practical advice and solutions based on your own experiences. Encourage them to set SMART goals and create action plans to achieve them. Provide ongoing support and motivation to keep them on track.

Remember, mentoring is a two-way street. While you are guiding and inspiring others, you also have the opportunity to learn and grow from their perspectives and experiences. Embrace the opportunity to build meaningful relationships and create a network of like-minded individuals who can support and uplift each other.

8.4.3 Giving Back to the Community

Paying it forward goes beyond mentoring individuals. It also involves giving back to the community and making a positive impact on a larger scale. As a small business owner, you have the power to contribute to causes that align with your values and mission.

Consider partnering with local charities or nonprofit organizations that are making a difference in your community. Donate a portion of your profits or organize fundraising events to support their initiatives. By aligning your business with a greater purpose, you not only inspire others but also create a positive brand image and attract customers who share your values.

Additionally, you can share your expertise and knowledge through workshops, seminars, or webinars. Offer free or discounted training sessions to aspiring entrepreneurs or individuals who are looking to enhance their skills. By providing valuable resources and education, you empower others to pursue their dreams and create their own success stories.

8.4.4 Cultivating a Culture of Inspiration

Inspiring others and paying it forward should not be limited to external interactions. It's equally important to cultivate a culture of inspiration within your own business. By creating an environment that fosters growth, collaboration, and support, you can empower your employees to reach their full potential and contribute to the success of your business.

Encourage open communication and idea-sharing among your team members. Recognize and celebrate their achievements and milestones. Provide opportunities for professional development and growth. By investing in the growth and success of your employees, you create a positive and inspiring work environment that attracts top talent and fosters loyalty.

In conclusion, as someone who has mastered the art of goal achievement, it is your responsibility to inspire others and pay it forward. By sharing your knowledge, becoming a mentor, giving back to the community, and cultivating a culture of inspiration within your own business, you can create a lasting impact and contribute to the success and fulfillment of others. Remember, success is not just about personal achievements, but also about the positive influence you have on others.